Two in the Bush

Gerald Durrell

Two in the Bush

Illustrations by B. L. Driscoll

New York · The Viking Press

Copyright © 1966 by Gerald Durrell

Viking Compass Edition
issued in 1971 by The Viking Press, Inc.
625 Madison Avenue, New York, N. Y. 10022

SBN 670-73674-0 (hardbound)
    670-00334-4 (paperbound)

Library of Congress catalog card number: 66-23821

Printed in the United States of America

For
CHRIS AND JIM
In memory of
Leeches, Lyrebirds and the
Bicycle in the Chimney
(not to mention the Glow-worms)

CONTENTS

A WORD IN ADVANCE

THIS IS THE CHRONICLE of a six month journey which took us through New Zealand, Australia and Malaya. The reasons for this journey were twofold —firstly that I wanted to see what was being done about conservation in these countries, and secondly that the BBC wanted to make a series of television films on the same subject. I am acutely conscious of the fact that the length of time we spent in each country gives the impression of an extremely rapid Cook's tour and, quite obviously, I have probably misshapen the truth and left out a number of things which I should have mentioned.

It is, strangely enough, very difficult to write a book like this and try to strike a happy medium between a work entitled *Two and a Half Days in Djakarta* or *South East Asia Exposed* and to write the literal truth, as you see it, which may appear offensive to the many people who gave you such unstinting help and such warm hospitality; people unfortunately have a habit of taking things personally.

So may I take this opportunity to fend off a few of the irate letters which I will inevitably receive from New Zealanders, Australians and Malayans, telling me that no one who has spent only six weeks in the country has the right to criticise. I think that having spent five minutes in a place you have every right to criticise. Whether your criticisms are valid or not is for the reader to decide. But at any rate, I can say one thing with all honesty—that it was a glorious trip and I enjoyed every moment of it.

I

LAND OF THE
LONG WHITE CLOUD

He had forty-two boxes, all carefully packed,
With his name printed clearly on each.

Hunting of the Snark

THE ARRIVAL

WE *had* meant to creep unobtrusively into New Zealand, film and see what we wanted to, and then creep unobtrusively out again. But when the ship docked at Auckland, we found that the Wildlife Department—having been appraised of our arrival—had unrolled a red carpet of embarrassing dimensions for us. The first intimation of this was the arrival on board of a short, stocky individual (looking not unlike a muscular Tweedle Dum) with round, innocent baby-blue eyes and a wide grin.

'I,' he proclaimed, crushing my hand in an iron grasp, 'am Brian Bell of the Wildlife Service. The Department has given me the job of escorting you round New Zealand and making sure that you see all you want to see.'

'That's extremely kind of the Department,' I said, 'but I had really no intention of worrying . . .'

'I have driven your Land-Rover up from Wellington,' interrupted Brian firmly, 'and yesterday I met your two colleagues from the BBC and they are on their way up to meet us.'

'That's very kind . . .' I began.

'Also,' continued Brian as if I had not spoken, fixing me with his hypnotic blue stare, 'I have worked out an itinerary for you. Just cross out the things you don't want to do.'

He handed me a sheaf of typewritten documents that looked

like a cross between the plans for a Royal State Visit and some gigantic army manoeuvres. It was full of fascinating suggestions and orders, such as 'June five, 0500 hours, see Royal Albatross, Taiaroa Head.' Had the Albatross, I wondered dazedly, been issued with a similar itinerary and, if so, would they fly past in formation and dip their wings in salute? But in spite of these intriguing thoughts, I was a bit alarmed for I did not want my trip to New Zealand to degenerate into that hideous thing, the conducted tour. However, before I could voice an opinion on the matter, Brian had glanced at his watch, scowled terrifyingly, muttered to himself and then disappeared at a smart trot. I was leaning against the rail, clutching my massive itinerary and feeling slightly dazed, when Jacquie appeared.

'Who was that bloke in the brown suit I saw you talking to?' she asked.

'That was one Brian Bell,' I replied, handing her the itinerary. 'He's from the Wildlife Department and he has been sent especially to Organise us with a capital O.'

'I thought that's just what you wanted to avoid?' said Jacquie.

'It was,' I said gloomily.

She glanced rapidly through the itinerary and raised her eyebrows.

'How long do they think we're staying—ten years?' she asked.

At that moment Brian returned and I introduced him to Jacquie.

'Pleased to meet you,' he said absently. 'Now, all your luggage has gone ashore and I have arranged Customs clearance. We'll load it up and drive to the hotel. The first Press Conference I've arranged for eleven o'clock and the second one for two-thirty. Then there's the TV interview tonight, but we needn't worry about that *yet*. So if you're ready, we can get started.'

Our minds in a whirl, we were hustled ashore by Brian and the next few hours were among the most hectic I have ever spent. When we arrived at the hotel Brian handed us over to the Government PRO, Terry Egan, a small man with a humorous, carunculated face and a pleasant wit.

'I'll leave you with Terry,' said Brian, 'and see you later. I've got a bit more Organising to do.'

What was he going to Organise, I wondered? A Guard of Honour consisting of ten thousand Kiwis to line the streets as we left Auckland? In the very short time I had known Brian Bell I felt that he might be capable of Organising even this. So Brian left us, and hardly had he disappeared when the first gaggle of reporters arrived. After that, things became increasingly chaotic. We were photographed from every conceivable angle and our most fatuous statements treated with the reverence that would be accorded to the utterances of a couple of sages. Then came a welcome but all too brief pause for lunch, and the whole thing started all over again. Late in the afternoon, as the last of the reporters left, I turned to Terry as a drowning man might turn to a straw.

'Terry,' I implored hoarsely, 'isn't there a nice, quiet place we can go and have a drink and not *talk* for ten minutes or so . . . some peaceful Nirvana where reporters are not allowed?'

'Yes,' said Terry promptly, 'I can jack that up . . . know the very place.'

'Well, while you have a drink I'll go and have a bath,' said Jacquie.

'Okay, we won't be long,' I said. 'I just want something to soothe my shattered nerves. If anyone else asks me what I think of New Zealand, I shall scream.'

'Yes,' said Jacquie, 'what did you say to that female reporter who asked you that? I couldn't hear.'

'He said that he thought the little bit of the docks that he'd seen were very pretty,' said Terry chuckling.

'You shouldn't *say* things like that,' said Jacquie.

'Well, it was a silly question and it deserved a silly answer.'

'Come on,' said Terry, 'we both need a drink.'

I followed Terry out of the hotel and down the street. We turned several corners and then came to a brown door, through which Terry dived. I followed him thirstily into what I thought was going to be a haven of peace and tranquillity.

I shall always attribute my uncertain start in New Zealand to the fact that I was introduced too early to what is known as 'the five o'clock swill'. The phrase has, when you consider it, a wonderful pastoral—one might almost say idyllic—ring to it. It conjures up a picture of fat but hungry porcines, all freshly scrubbed, eagerly and gratefully partaking of their warm mash from the horny but kindly hands of a jovial farmer, a twinkling-eyed son of the soil.

Nothing could be further from the truth.

The five o'clock swill is the direct result of New Zealand's imbecilic licencing laws. In order to prevent people from getting drunk the pubs close at six, just after the office workers leave work. This means that they have to leave their place of employment, rush frantically to the nearest pub, and make a desperate attempt to drink as much beer as they can in the shortest possible time. As a means of cutting down on drunkenness, this is quite one of the most illogical deterrents I have come across.

The Haven of Peace that Terry had lured me into was just in the process of dishing out the five o'clock swill, and the scene was almost indescribable. Dozens of thirsty New Zealanders lined the bar some twenty deep, all talking at the tops of their voices and gulping beer as fast as they could. To facilitate the replenishing of their glasses with all possible speed, the beer was served through a long hosepipe with a tap on the end. As the empty glasses were slapped on the counter, the man behind the bar moved rapidly up and down squirting them full of beer. This was an operation fraught with difficulty, and more beer appeared to go on the counter than anywhere else. I was introduced to half a dozen people in rapid succession, none of whose names I caught, and they all promptly bought me a glass of beer. At one point I had eight glasses of beer in front of me and my hands were so occupied with holding another three glasses that I could no longer shake hands with anyone. Everyone, periodically— as if at a given signal—would shout, 'Drink up, drink up, they *close* in a minute.' With the combination of the beer and the noise my head started to ache. I managed to drink my eight glasses of beer and, like a hideous conjuring trick, another eight appeared in their place. New Zealand hospitality is generous, but exhausting. Then suddenly an enormous brass bell let out an ear-splitting clanging, like the distraught cries of a fire engine thwarted in love. I thought the pub must have caught fire and wondered hazily if they would put out the conflagration with a hosepipe full of beer. I found Terry looking at me mournfully.

'I'm sorry, Gerry, that's closing time,' he said with considerable sadness. 'We should have come earlier.'

'Yes, it's a shame,' I shouted back untruthfully.

We fought our way out into the street and staggered back to the hotel, where Terry left me. I found Jacquie looking revoltingly fresh and rested after her bath.

'Did you have a nice drink?' she asked.

I did not even deign to reply, but lay down on the bed and closed my eyes.

I was just drifting off into a pleasant doze when there was a knock on the door and Brian Bell appeared, with an Organising gleam in his eye.

'Hullo,' he said brightly, 'feeling more rested?'

'I feel,' I said bitterly, 'as if I had just been rescued by the skin of my teeth from an exceptionally large butt of Malmsey.'

'Good,' said Brian, not really listening. 'Now, as we have to make an early start tomorrow and as this will be your last chance to see them, I thought you might like to run down and see the Wrybills. We've got time before the TV show.'

One of the basic rules of life, I have found, is that you never learn anything unless you confess your ignorance. Say that you don't know and people fall over themselves to teach you or show you and within next to no time all is vouchsafed to you. I applied this philosophy now.

'What is a Wrybill?' I asked.

Brian's round blue eyes became even more rounded at this confession of my ignorance, but he was too polite to say anything.

'It's a small wading bird,' he explained carefully, as to a mentally defective child of two, 'and it gets its name from the fact that its beak is twisted to one side. They're only found in New Zealand and there are not very many of them left —I should think the total population is about 5,000 but we haven't done a proper count on them. There's a small colony of them just down the coast from here and I thought we could nip down and see them.'

The idea of seeing a bird with a beak that bent sideways, even to a naturalist in my condition, was irresistible, and so in a very short time we had left the outskirts of Auckland behind and were driving through the countryside. As we drove further and further a deep depression settled on me, for the landscape was exactly the pleasant, gently undulating type of countryside you can find on the Dorset-Devon borders: lush green grassy hillsides, daisy-speckled with flocks of sheep; small, neatly hedged fields, with their windbreaks of small copses; even the birds that flew up from the side of the road were starlings, blackbirds, thrushes, and high above us a skylark was hung, singing his evening song. To have travelled so far and so eagerly from England only to find yourself in another England seemed to me a refinement of torture which—on top of the beer—was almost unendurable. By the time we were bumping down a rough track towards the coast I was in a mood of black depression and was beginning to wonder why we had come to New Zealand in the first place. We might just as well have stayed at home if all we were going to see was blackbirds and skylarks.

Brian eased the Land-Rover through a flock of sheep who scattered before us, their fleeces wobbling as they ran, and then brought the vehicle to rest by a hedge. Beyond the hedge spread an area of rough, tussocky ground, beyond that a bare, flat area of dried mud, then a shingle beach and the grey uninviting sea. Normally, Brian explained, the Wry-bills spent their time feeding on a long shingle spit to the left of us, but at high tide, when the spit was covered, they moved inland to the flat muddy area that we could see directly in front of us. We strained our eyes but, as far as we could see, there was no bird life in sight. Brian, muttering the outraged mutters of an Organiser whose Organisation has broken down, moved slowly down the hedge and we followed him. A stiff, cold breeze had now sprung up, accompanied by a mild drizzle, and I began to think longing thoughts of warm baths and soft beds. Suddenly Brian stopped and lifted his field-glasses.

'Ha!' he barked triumphantly, '*there* they are. A little out of position, but they're *there*.'

He pointed and I focused my glasses at the area he indicated. At first all I could see was a large expanse of uninspiring grey mud, apparently completely devoid of any life whatsoever. Then I saw what at first glance appeared to be a grey, gossamer-like shawl of large dimensions, performing a sort of whirligig motion on the mud. On close examination this turned out to be a tightly packed conglomeration of small birds, all performing some strange gyrations that kept them in almost constant motion yet on exactly the same spot. The range was too far to see exactly what they were doing, so we moved cautiously through the tussocky area of rough ground that separated us from them, and eventually managed to get within about two hundred feet without apparently causing them the slightest alarm. Then we could see clearly what they were doing, and it was one of the most extraordinary group actions I have seen performed by birds.

The Wrybills were small (about the size of a Ringed Plover), bluish-grey on the upper parts and white below, with a white stripe across the forehead and across the top of the eye, and a very neat black bib under the chin. The small beaks were all bent from left to right like a bill-hook, and this, for some extraordinary reason, combined with their neatly domed heads and dark eyes, made them look as if they all had snub noses. But it was their actions that fascinated me even more than their unique beak formation. There were about fifty of them and they covered an area some thirty feet by twenty, all facing into the wind and all standing on one leg. I noticed that each bird kept some twelve inches or so away from its neighbours. They would stand there, shuffling their feathers and blinking, balancing their frail bodies against the wind, looking incredibly mournful. Then suddenly, and

—as far as I could see—for no particular reason, one of them would hop forward (still on one leg) some six inches or so. This would, of course, destroy the careful territory arrangement of the whole group, and so all the birds nearest to the one that had moved would have to move too and, in turn, all the ones nearest to *them* would have to move, and so on. Thus, periodically, the whole conglomeration would be in motion yet the group as a whole remained exactly where it was. However carefully I watched them I could not see any valid reason for this sudden outbreak of movement; they were not displaying, nor were they feeding. They just stood there like a group of dispirited, poverty-stricken orphans, and every so often—to relieve the tedium—they would break into this weird game of hopscotch. Brian said it was thought that the strange shape of the Wrybill's beak was to assist it in feeding. With this curious bent beak, it can slide it more easily under stones in search of the tiny crustaceans and other sea life on which it lives.

We watched the cold, shuffling, hopscotching crowd of Wrybills for about an hour, and during that time there had been immense activity within the group, yet the group as a whole had hardly moved more than a yard or so from where we had first seen them. Fascinating though they were to watch, time was getting short and so we reluctantly climbed back into the Land-Rover and drove back through fine drizzle into Auckland. I felt strangely comforted by my sight of the Wrybills; they were, I felt, an omen that perhaps we were going to see some interesting things in New Zealand after all.

CHAPTER I

Geysers, Wekas and Kakas

Should we meet with a Jubjub, that desperate bird,
We shall need all our strength for the job!

Hunting of the Snark

THE NEXT MORNING we rose at what I considered to be an inordinately early hour (I was still suffering from the effects of 'the swill') and we had soon left Auckland behind and were driving through the English-looking countryside, with the usual depressing glimpses of blackbirds, thrushes and starlings to enliven the landscape. Brian drove and did it, as he did all things, extremely well. Over the weeks that we were to get to know him, my liking and respect for him grew daily. He was quiet, resourceful and, above all, knew his job backwards. His chief concern was that what was left of New Zealand's indigenous wild life should not become extinct owing to sloppy or insufficient conservation laws or measures. As we drove along he explained to me the problems facing the Wildlife Department in its efforts to salvage what was left of the New Zealand fauna.

The first thing to remember, he explained, was that New Zealand—geologically speaking—is a very young country and so the majority of the rock formation is extremely soft. In places you can, literally, crumple the rock up in your hands. This soft rock is covered by a thin layer of topsoil, held in place by forests in most areas, and on the hilltops by various

grasses. The first to come to New Zealand were a race called the Moa Hunters, so called because they appear to have existed, to a large extent, by killing and eating the now extinct gigantic ostrich-like bird called the Moa. The Moa Hunters did not do tremendous damage to the forests, though they burnt and cut a certain amount. Then the Maoris arrived and proceeded to exterminate the Moa Hunters. The Maoris did considerably more damage to the forests and grasslands by burning and cutting. Then came the European and he carried on the good work with such thoroughness that soon vast areas were denuded of forest and grass, and great bald patches of erosion started to appear. One of the first things the early settlers did (and certainly one of the stupidest) was to start introducing animals and birds, mainly from the 'Old Country'. Up until then nature (who, by and large, knows her job pretty well) had worked out a nice balance of the fauna. There were no mammals except a few bats, a few species of small, colourful and harmless reptiles, and a host of lovely birds. New Zealand, before the coming of man and particularly the European, was a paradise for birds: thick forests, grasslands, abundant insect life and virtually no predators. Into this harmonious paradise the European introduced blackbirds, thrushes, starlings, mallard, Mute Swan, skylark, pheasant, greenfinch, hedge sparrow, house sparrow, chaffinch, goldfinch and yellowhammer, to name only a few European species, together with more exotic ones like Indian Mynahs, White-Backed Magpies, Rosella Parrots and Black Swans. Not content with this act of criminal stupidity, they introduced the following mammals: Red Deer, Fallow Deer, Japanese Deer, Virginia Deer, Bush Wallabies, Chamois, Moose, Sambar, Possum, Thar, Wapiti, Javan Rusa. In the meantime, of course, the settlers continued to cut down the forest and overgraze the hillsides. So, with their habitat being decimated, and faced with competition from strange, introduced creatures with which they had never had to contend before, it is small wonder that a number of wonderful New Zealand birds became extinct and that all the other species, by and large, started to decline. Many unique bird species inhabited small islands off the coast and, even when unmolested, their total population could never have been very high. Many of these were exterminated by the deliberate or accidental introduction of cats that ran wild, or of sheep and goats that also became feral and devoured the vegetation, thus destroying the birds' habitat. Even now, Brian told me, the Wildlife Department was having an uphill struggle to try and rid the islands of these pests before some species of bird life gave up the unequal struggle. As we drove along Brian kept pointing out to me various examples of the sort of thing he meant, to underline his points.

'Look at that,' he would say, pulling up by the side of the road and pointing at a hillside, which, denuded of grass and in consequence of topsoil, had started to avalanche the soft rock into the valley below, 'that's a bit of over-grazing. They're not supposed to graze sheep over a thousand feet, but they do. Then you get *that*: grass goes, topsoil goes, rock crumbles and swoosh! Straight down into the valley. This causes a flash flood further down which rips the topsoil off the valley surface where it *should* have been safe.'

Or again, he would stop by the edge of the forest and show us where the young saplings had been 'ringed' by the introduced deer, that is to say, they had nibbled the tender bark off right round the trunk of the tree, thus killing it. But probably the most ironical sight he showed us were the telegraph and electricity poles, each wearing, halfway up, a sort of collar of zinc nailed to the pole.

'That,' said Brian, 'is for the Possums. Some bright cove

thought that Possums had nice skins so he'd start up a fur business. He imported his stock from Australia and started. The business failed, of course, so he let the Possums go. They're now a major pest. Not only do they eat hell out of the trees—they eat the buds and new shoots as well as the bark—but they took to climbing the electricity poles and getting themselves electrocuted and plunging whole towns into darkness. So they had to fit these metal collars on the poles so they can't climb up.'

By ten o'clock we reached a small town that lay on the edge of Lake Whangape, where we were supposed to meet Chris Parsons, the producer, and Jim Saunders, the cameraman. But as we drew up outside a small café near the lake there was no sign of them and Brian scowled at his watch.

'Can't understand it,' he said worriedly, 'they should have been here by now.'

'Perhaps they've gone down to the lake?' I suggested.

'They may have done,' said Brian doubtfully, 'but I said we'd meet them outside this café. Anyway, let's go and have a look.'

We left the Rover and made our way to the top of the grassy hillside that looked out over the lake, and in the bright sunlight, under a clear blue sky, it was a gorgeous sight. The lake itself was really like two or three large lakes, joined together by fairly narrow 'necks' of water and dotted with a variety of tree- and reed-covered islands. The gently undulating countryside around the shores of the lake was vivid emerald green, studded here and there with stands of poplar trees that were just starting to be toasted by the sun to a rich gold. But it was the surface of the lake that caught and held my attention, for on it floated such a vast concourse of Black Swans that I was speechless at the numbers. Some swam singly, others in great flotillas, and periodically a group of them would take wing in a leisurely fashion and fly after their reflections across the smooth surface of the water. There were so many of them that it was impossible even to try to make a rough count of their numbers; everywhere you looked there were swans swimming or flying, so that the whole surface of the lake was in constant motion. That such a vast concentration of birds found enough to eat, even on such large stretches of water, was incredible.

'We reckon,' said Brian laconically, 'that there are about ten thousand swans on this lake. Periodically, of course, we organise shoots to keep their numbers under some sort of control, but it's an uphill struggle.'

'I suppose if it wasn't for such vast quantities of these Australian interlopers the lake would be full of New Zealand duck?' I asked.

Brian shrugged.

'Yes,' he said, 'it would be a good lake for duck, but that's the trouble with New Zealand, as I told you. We introduced these damned things and now they've got out of control. This is one of the Department's biggest problems.'

The first Black Swan had been imported to New Zealand from Australia in 1864 and, judging by the surface of the lake lying below us, they had done no mean task of establishing themselves in their new environment. The main trouble with these beautiful and graceful swans is that they feed close to the shore—mainly on aquatic plants—and naturally they can reach these at greater depths than the ducks can. So, by starving the ducks and by fouling the water and the shore-line, they drive the ducks away. On the lake below us there was not a single duck, nothing but Black Swans as far as the eye could see.

My meditations on the stupidity of mankind were interrupted by the sound of an engine and when we scrambled down the hillside to the road, we found Chris and Jim just decanting themselves from a car.

'What ho! What ho!' shouted Chris in an unprecedented fit of exuberance, as he hurried down the road to meet us. He is a man of medium height with dark hair, green, rather heavily lidded eyes, and a nose that makes that of the late Duke of Wellington pale into insignificance. Normally of a quiet, self-effacing nature, he was now flushed with enthusiasm at this, his first major trip abroad, and he wrung our hands vigorously. Jim, the cameraman, was short and dark, with one of those rather handsome, finely etched faces you see on Roman medallions, and the most mischievous and disarming grin imaginable. He spoke with a faint, pleasant West Country burr to his voice, one of those attractive English accents that reminds one of comfortable things like drowsy beehives at dusk and cool apple orchards on a hot summer day.

'Well, well, *well*,' said Chris, still beaming with a self-satisfied air, as though he had created New Zealand himself. 'If anyone had told me eight weeks ago that we would meet on the shores of Lake Whangape, in the middle of New Zealand, exactly on time . . .'

'You aren't on time,' said Brian sternly, 'you're half an hour late.'

'We weren't,' said Chris indignantly, 'we arrived half an hour ago but as you all weren't here we've been up the road, shooting some wide angle shots of the lake.'

'Oh,' said Brian, slightly mollified, 'well, let's all have a cup of tea and then we can go down to the lake.'

Over a pot of tea and a huge pile of toast, Chris and I discussed what shape the filming should take when we went down to the lake. The theme of the programmes we were going to try to make was, of course, conservation. We wanted to show what was being done to preserve wild life in the countries we visited, and try to point out the necessity for conservation, not only of the animals but of their environment as well. As all the countries we were to visit were new to me, this presented quite a problem, for as soon as we arrived I had to try to get as much information about conservation as possible so that I could work out a rough shooting script for Chris and Jim to work from.

'In the trip down from Auckland I've tried to pick Brian's brains fairly thoroughly and as I see it the problems we ought to try and present are these,' I said. 'Firstly, the incredibly stupid introduction of foreign animals to New Zealand, most of which have become major pests—the Black Swans down there are a good example—and secondly, the altering of environment so that it affects both man and animal—the wholesale cutting down of the forests, as has happened in the past, and the overgrazing of the grasslands, as is happening now. I'll rough out a script of some sort on those lines tonight, but I think we ought to get some stuff on the swans because they *are* introduced, they *are* a pest and, at the same time, they're very spectacular and extremely graceful. What d'you think?'

Chris, as he always did when he was thinking, lidded his eyes like a hawk, retreated behind his nose and adopted an expression like a dispeptic Llama.

'Um,' he said at last, 'I'd like to see the script first but obviously, as you say, the introduced species which have turned into pests are going to play an important role, so I think we should get as much stuff on the swans as we can.'

'They've got Black Swans at Bristol Zoo,' said Jim through a mouthful of toast, 'we could have filmed them there . . . no need to come rushing out to New Zealand . . . waste of money . . . quick trip to Bristol Zoo and Bob's your uncle.'

'Take no notice of him,' said Chris with dignity. 'Cameramen are, by and large, an uncouth lot.'

'Ah-ha!' said Jim, 'but at least I *know* I'm uncouth—that's a saving grace, that is. Know yourself, that's what I say. Look at Chris here, goes through life full of faults and doesn't recognise one of 'em. What I say is, enjoy your faults while you may. Who knows, tomorrow someone may come along and reform you and then where would you be?'

'They'd have an uphill struggle trying to reform *you*,' said Chris crushingly.

Presently we drove down a rough track to the edge of the lake where the Warden was waiting beside a large boat driven by a powerful outboard engine. We unpacked the camera gear and the recording apparatus and piled it into the boat; Henry started the engine and we were away, skimming swiftly across the smooth waters of the lake towards the biggest concentration of swans. The first shots we wanted to get were of the swans taking wing, as we thought this would show their impressive numbers to advantage, so Henry headed the boat towards an area of the lake surface where the water was scarcely visible for the thick mass of swans, revved up the engine to full speed and then, when we were about a hundred yards or so away from the nearest swans, shut off the engine and let the boat plough on under its own momentum. The great concourse of birds were all swimming away from us as rapidly as they could, but they could not compete in speed with the boat and very soon a few of the more nervous ones took wing. This spread panic and within a few seconds something like five or six hundred swans were all desperately trying to get off the water. With their ash grey and black plumage and their sealing-wax red beaks and feet, they were a splendid sight as they churned up the still waters in their take-off and then, as they rose and circled over us, the noise of their wing-beats was like the applause of an immense audience in a gigantic, echoing concert hall. They flew over us, necks stretched out, like hundreds of black crosses in the sky, their white wingtips flashing against the dark plumage of their bodies like lights. Soon the blue sky above the lake was full of wheeling swans, like a great burst of black confetti, and it was frightening to watch this pageant of birds and realise that they were the outcome of the careless introduction of just a few pairs a little over a hundred years ago. As an example of how man blunders when he starts interfering with nature, it could not have been more impressive.

We zoomed to and fro over the surface of the lake and came across several younger swans who were quite determined that we were not going to panic them into flight. They would swim along in a sedate and correct swan-like fashion, wings folded carefully to show the curious, scalloped ruff of feathers where they lay along the body, neck curved in just the right elegant S shape. But gradually, as the boat began to overtake them, they would start to get nervous: they would hold their wings further and further away from their bodies and their necks would gradually droop until they were stretched out in a straight line. Then, as the boat got nearer still, they would utter honks of dismay, churn the water with wild wing-beats, and take off at last in a welter of foam, trailing their brilliant red legs as they became airborne.

At last we had got all the film we needed and we headed back to the shore. We had hardly moored before the whirling black clouds of swans were settling once more on the surface of the lake, arrowing the dark waters as they landed. We packed up the gear, feeling reasonably happy at the shots we had managed to obtain, and then, after another enormous pot of tea, and toast, started on the next leg of our journey. Our destination was a town called Rotorua and it must surely be one of the most curious as well as one of the most unsafe towns in the world, for the whole town is built on what is, to all intents and purposes, a breeding ground for volcanoes.

The town, as you enter it, looks—as so many New Zealand towns do—like a Hollywood set for a cowboy film. You feel that if you went round the backs of the wooden houses fronting the main street, you would find that they *had* no backs. But the most noticeable thing about Rotorua as you enter it is the smell, a smell that you first attribute to a million rotting eggs but which, after the first two or three glorious lungfuls, you realise is pure sulphur. To anyone with a sensitive nose the smell is so strong you almost feel you can touch it. Then other rather ominous signs show you that this town is different from others. At various points along the pavements, or even in the middle of the road, you will see a crack in the macadam through which a jet of white steam is puffing merrily, as though it were the site of the premature burial of a small steam engine. This adds a certain macabre attraction to the street scenes but it can have its dangerous side as well. Shortly before we arrived, Brian told us, a man was trying to do some renovations to his cellars when a swing of his pickaxe unleashed a jet of boiling steam that killed him. In his enthusiasm he had punctured what might be called a major artery of a volcano and had died in consequence. Jim, on hearing this story, voted loudly and vociferously that we press on to the next town and not stay overnight in Rotorua as we had planned, but he was overruled.

'You're all mad,' he said with conviction, 'you mark my words, we'll all wake up in bed tomorrow like boiled halibut. And the *smell*—how do you expect me to eat with this smell? Everything will taste the same.'

I must say that he was perfectly right in this contention,

for all the food we ate in Rotorua had a strong but unmistakable flavour of rotting eggs. But then, as I pointed out, the food in the average New Zealand hotel would, if anything, be improved by the flavour of sulphur.

When we had found our board and lodging for the night, Brian took us down to what he kept calling the 'thermal springs' and I can't say that I was particularly keen to see them, for the term—for me at any rate—conjured up some of the more frightful places I have been to during my life, where ancient and decrepit men and women propel themselves from spring to spring in bath chairs, hawking and spitting and imbibing the most revolting water that well (or so it smells) from the very bowels of the earth. To anyone who thinks that witchcraft is dead, a short sojourn in one of these watering places is extremely instructive. However, Brian's idea of thermal springs and mine, I soon found, were totally different, and I would not have missed it for anything, for what he showed us was quite incredible. We drove to the edge of the town, left the Land-Rover and made our way down into a valley. Immediately the smell of rotting eggs intensified a thousand-fold and the air seemed to be damper and warmer. Then, round a corner of the path, it was as though we had suddenly been transported back millions of years to the days when the earth was still young, unformed and uncooled. Here the rocks had folded and twisted into strange shapes, and through holes and splits in their surface jets of steam—some small, some six or eight feet high—gushed forth at intervals, as blood spurts out of a cut artery, obeying some strange pulse in the earth's depths. Through every little fissure in the rocks tiny wisps of steam curled sluggishly, so the air was filled with moisture and you viewed everything through a shifting veil of steam. Some of the bigger geysers —twelve or fourteen feet in height—would keep up a steady column of steam for some ten minutes or so, mysteriously die away and then, after a pause, suddenly shoot forth again with a strange hooting, whistling sound. If you happened to be standing over the blowhole at that precise moment the results could have been fatal, since even the spray from these columns of boiling steam was well above average bath temperature.

We picked our way across this slippery and somewhat dangerous terrain until we came to the banks of a small stream that babbled eagerly over its bed of stones wearing a shifting coat of steam, the water being a reasonable ninety-odd degrees. Crossing this, we made our way further down the valley and suddenly came upon the mud holes, which to me were so fascinating that they kept me absorbed for the next half hour. These pools varied in size: some covered quite large areas, others were only the circumference of a small table, and they varied in colour, some being pale *café-au-lait* and others a rich, dark brown. The mud in these pools was the consistency and colour of boiling milk chocolate, and boiling was exactly what it appeared to be doing. In actual fact the mud, although warm, was not boiling but gave this impression because of the small jets of steam that had to force their way to the surface through this glutinous mass. The surface of a pool would be smooth and unblemished, looking good enough to dip a spoon into and eat; then suddenly this placid surface would be disturbed by a bubble that would form—a tiny bubble the size of a blackbird's egg. Very slowly this would rise above the surface and grow until it was the size of a ping-pong ball or even the size of an orange if the consistency of the mud was thick enough. Then it would burst, with a curiously loud 'Glup' noise, and form a miniature moon crater which would slowly be absorbed back into the smooth surface of the pool until the next build-up of steam repeated the performance. In some pools where the steam was pushing through fairly rapidly, you would get little bevies of bubbles, sometimes as many as six or seven, forming in a circle and—as it were—singing together. It reminded me rather of bell-ringing, for the bubbles were not all of the same size and so they made different noises as they burst and, as the steam was coming through at regular intervals, you got these groups of fat bubbles playing tunes: Glop . . . plip . . . Glug . . . plip . . . Splop . . . plip . . . Glug . . . plish . . . Splop . . . plip . . . and so on. It was fascinating, and I crouched over the mud pools completely absorbed in these bubble orchestras. I had just found a particularly talented group of seventeen who were playing something so harmonious and complicated that I was convinced it had been written by Bach, and was working out a scheme whereby I could get them to sign a contract so that I could take them back to England to appear at the Festival Hall (perhaps with Sir Malcolm Sargent conducting), when I was brought rudely back to earth by Chris, who appeared out of the mist looking like a slightly distraught Dante.

'Come along, dear boy,' he said, 'stop playing mud pies. I've got six geysers lined up, all spouting like anything, and I want to get a shot of you and Jacquie walking along in front of them.'

'You do get the most charming ideas!' I said bitterly, as I tore myself away from the singing bubbles and followed him into the mists.

Sure enough, there were six geysers, each some twelve to fourteen feet high, almost in a row, all spouting merrily and uttering hoots and whistles to each other.

'There,' said Chris proudly. 'Now, what I want Jacquie and you to do is walk from that rock *there*, across the front of them and stop about *there*.'

'Do we get danger money?' enquired Jacquie. Her dark hair was covered with a fine mist of tiny water droplets, so she looked as though she had gone prematurely grey.

'You only get danger money if Big Bertha goes off,' said Chris, grinning.

'What is Big Bertha?' I enquired.

Chris pointed to a fairly large hole in the rock surface not far from the area he wanted us to walk across.

'Big Bertha's in that hole,' he explained. 'She's apparently the largest of the geysers here but she only goes off at irregular intervals, about once every ten or fifteen years. When she really gets going she's about fifty foot high, they say. Must be quite a sight.' There was a wistful note in his voice, and I fixed him with a stern eye.

'Let us be quite clear about this,' I said, 'I have not the slightest intention of mucking about with a fifty foot geyser under any circumstances!'

Jacquie and I made our way to the spot Chris had pointed out and waited patiently until the camera and sound recording equipment was ready; then, at a signal from Chris, we started to walk across the rocks, the small geysers behind us spouting vigorously and making quite an impressive sight.

We were halfway across when the ground started to tremble under our feet, there was a noise like a gargantuan belch followed by a hiss, and a jet of boiling steam the circumference of a medium-sized tree trunk suddenly vomited forth from Big Bertha's blow-hole and towered above us. It climbed higher and higher, the hissing getting louder, and then the top curved over like a fountain and rained scalding drops of water on us. Throwing discretion to the winds, Jacquie and I turned and ran. In fact, apart from the time I was chased by an infuriated Gnu, I can never remember having run so fast. We arrived, panting, at the place where Chris and Jim were leaping up and down with excitement and Brian was standing with a broad, proud grin on his face as if he had personally Organised Big Bertha.

'Wonderful,' shouted Chris above the hissing of Big Bertha, 'simply *wonderful*—it couldn't have been better.'

Jacquie and I sat down on a damp rock to recover our breath and gazed at each other.

'Such an interesting life you lead, Mr. Durrell,' she said. 'How I envy you.'

'Yes, it's one endless round of thrills and pleasure,' I said, wiping the water off my face and endeavouring to light a cigarette with a sodden match.

'I don't know what you're complaining about,' said Chris, 'you were well clear of it.'

'That,' I said, 'is not the point. You assured me that the bloody thing only went off once a century or something. Suppose I had, in a fit of boyish enthusiasm, decided to go and stand over that hole? It would have been the enema to end all enemas.'

While Chris and Jim took a few more shots of Big Bertha from different angles, Jacquie and I went back and played with the mud pools, and then presently we packed up the equipment and climbed out of the valley. At the top I paused and looked back at the twisted and tortured rock formation, the columns of hissing steam and the gleaming area of the mud pools, all seen dimly now through the thickening mist that Big Bertha's eruption had caused. It looked like an illustration by Gustave Doré and I would not have been surprised to see a dinosaur suddenly appear round a shoulder of rock on its way for a quick dip in a mud pool.

After the night at Rotorua (during which we were not boiled in our beds, as Jim had so mournfully predicted) we set off once again down towards Wellington, at the tip of North

Island. After a few hours of driving, when we were all getting bored with suddenly shouting 'Look!' only to find it was a hedge sparrow or a chaffinch, Brian drove us down a road that led along the shores of a large and placid lake surrounded by tall stands of timber, and here at last we started to see some New Zealand birds. The lake was, of course, heavily besprinkled with its quota of Black Swans, but there was not a sufficient concentration of them to have completely eliminated the indigenous wildfowl and so we leapt out of the Land-Rover with enthusiasm, armed with cameras and binoculars, and were soon all busy with our different tasks: Chris and Jim filming, Jacquie, Brian and I watching the birds, while Brian identified them for us and gave us a thumbnail portrait of their distribution and habits. By far the commonest and most beautiful were the Paradise Ducks, several pairs of which were feeding in the shallow water within thirty or forty feet of us. One of the most extraordinary things about them was the difference between the male and the female; at first glance they looked like two totally unrelated species. The male had the head, neck and breast shining black; the back was also black, but delicately pencilled with white lines, and the underside was a rich fox red, also pencilled with fine white lines. In complete contrast, the female had the back black, as in the male, pencilled with white, the breast and underside fox red with white lines, and a completely white head and neck. Never having seen these beautiful ducks before, I was under the impression that the female was the male, since her colouring made her stand out so dominantly, until Brian disillusioned me. It still seems to be a curious thing that the female should be so much more conspicuous than the male for she, after all, has the hazardous job of sitting on the nest, when you would have thought that camouflage was an essential. Next to the Paradise Duck the other commonest New

Zealand species was the Black Teal, but these were much more wary and swam in small groups way out on the lake, so we had to content ourselves with getting glimpses of them with our binoculars. They were neat, compact little birds with rather short, stubby beaks, and they swam in a swift and rather furtive manner. The head and neck were black, with a purplish sheen above and a greenish one below, while what you could see of their body above the waterline was black. This rather sombre plumage was nicely set off by a white band on the wing, the slate blue beak and a bright yellow eye.

After we had spent several hours pleasantly occupied, by the lake, we climbed into the Land-Rover and continued our journey to Wellington. Here we were booked in at a hotel which, like all the other New Zealand hotels we had so far inhabited, left practically everything to be desired. We met with such pure, unadulterated kindness from everyone in New Zealand during our stay that it made our reception in the hotels worse by contrast.

Rising early the next morning we drove down towards the coast. Brian had insisted that before we left North Island we visit Kapiti, a tiny island lying off the coast, which was a bird sanctuary. Tired by my constant moaning about blackbirds and thrushes, he had assured me that on Kapiti I really would see a good cross section of native New Zealand birds. So we reached the coast and parked the Land-Rover alongside a stretch of sandy beach on which gentle rollers were breaking. Directly before us lay Kapiti, a long, hump-backed island thickly covered with trees and looking, in the pale morning light, dark and grim and not the slightest bit inviting. Jim gazed at the creaming rollers and then measured the distance between the shore and the island.

'How do we get out there?' he asked nervously. 'Swim?'

'No, no. George Fox—he's the Warden of the island—is going to pick us up in his launch,' said Brian, glancing at his watch. 'He should be here any minute now.'

We unloaded all the equipment and piled it along the sea wall in readiness, and presently we saw the tiny shape of the launch leave the edge of the island and come bouncing over the rollers towards us. Jim viewed its exuberant progress with increasing alarm.

'I shall be sick,' he announced in a sepulchral voice.

'Nonsense,' said Chris, 'it's not rough—and anyway, you can't be sick over such a short distance.'

'I was once sick in an army lorry crossing the Rhine,' said Jim with immense dignity.

There was a short pause while we all assimilated this extraordinary statement.

'I have no wish to appear more ignorant than I am,' I said carefully, 'but I fail to see how you can be sick in an army lorry crossing the Rhine—what was it, an amphibious lorry?'

'No,' said Jim, 'it was on a pontoon bridge, see? And as we were going across the pontoon bridge kept going up and down.'

'Well?' prompted Chris, fascinated.

'So I was sea-sick,' said Jim simply.

Silently I wrung his hand.

'I am proud,' I said, 'to meet a man who has enough courage to be sea-sick crossing a river on a pontoon bridge in an army lorry. No wonder we won the war.'

By this time the launch was nosing its way through the small breakers at the shoreline and it grounded in the sand with a gentle scrunch. George Fox appeared out of the tiny wheelhouse, leapt over the side and waded ashore to greet us. He was a short, stocky man with a brown, weatherbeaten face and clear blue eyes. His manner was reserved, almost taciturn, but I was to learn later that this was not his usual approach to people. It was simply that, in the past, he had had many naturalists invading his island to see his birds, and for the most part they appeared to have been a boorish lot. So naturally each fresh consignment of nature lovers and film makers was treated by George with a certain amount of suspicion until they had proved themselves.

The launch bounced merrily over the half mile or so of water that separated Kapiti from the mainland, and Jim sat grimly in the wheelhouse with an expression of foreboding on his face. However, we reached the tiny landing stage before any major disaster overtook him. At close sight the island looked even more forbidding than it had done from the mainland. The hillside rose sheer above us, covered with dark green beech forest that seemed uncannily silent and deserted. We unloaded the equipment and humped it up a narrow path up the hillside and, as we walked through the dense, gloomy forest, the drumming began.

At first it sounded as though a pigmy, hidden somewhere in the undergrowth to our left, was belting out a gentle tattoo on a tiny tom-tom. The sound lasted a few seconds and then stopped. After a short pause, it was replied to by another pigmy concealed somewhere on our right: a brief tattoo and then silence. Suddenly, as if some message had been received and understood, the tom-toms started throbbing all around us, working out complicated patterns of sound, questioning and answering each other in an intricate conversation.

'When do the pigmies attack?' I asked Brian, for it really sounded as though these were drums working some minute tribe up into a warlike frenzy. Brian grinned.

' I told you you'd see some real New Zealand birds here,' he said. 'Those are the Wekas. One of the most inquisitive birds in New Zealand. They always want to know who's arrived on the island and what they're up to. You'll see them in a minute.'

We continued up the path and then suddenly came out into a sun-filled clearing in which stood George Fox's neat little bungalow. Here we were greeted by his sister, who immediately won all our hearts by offering us hot coffee and home-made cakes As we sat outside in the sunshine, gorging ourselves on this most welcome repast, I suddenly saw a brown head appear from behind a rock, peer at me interestedly with large, dark eyes and then disappear.

'Brian,' I said, 'a brown bird just poked its head out from behind that rock.'

'Yes,' said Brian through a mouthful of cake, 'that was a Weka. They'll all be here in a minute. They can't resist anything new.'

As Brian said this another brown head appeared out of some undergrowth, regarded us with a knowing look and then carefully retreated. They kept peeping at us like this for some

time, now from behind a rock, now from the depths of a
patch of ferns, but after a few minutes of this intensive
scrutiny they decided that we were harmless, and then, like
a conjuring trick, we were suddenly surrounded by Wekas.
They clustered around us (appearing from the most unlikely
places) and examined all the camera equipment minutely,
pecking gently at the leather cases and the tin boxes full of
film, regarding the tripods with their heads on one side, and
all the time keeping up an endless tom-tom conversation with
each other, for all the world as if they were Customs Officers
who suspected us of smuggling. They were handsome if
somewhat sombre-looking birds that reminded me of extremely large Corncrakes. They had a typical rail-like walk, placing
their large feet rather carefully on the ground as if they
suffered from corns, and with the head and neck stretched out
in an inquisitive fashion. Their top half was a nice autumnal
rufous colour, spotted here and there with black, while the
throat and underside, together with a dashing stripe over the
eye, were grey. The beak was reddish, like the feet, and the
eye, which had looked quite dark from a distance, now turned
out to be an attractive reddish-brown.

Having given the equipment the once-over they then
approached us and investigated our clothing and shoes, pecking at our feet very gently and moving to and fro among
us in the most sedate fashion, still thrumming away to each
other. This noise, when heard at close range, had an extraordinary ventriloquial quality: the Weka at your feet
would drum suddenly and you could see him doing it, yet
the sound appeared to come from some distance away. In
spite of their placidity we soon found that a handful of cake
crumbs scattered on the path brought on the most disgraceful
free-for-all, with much barging and shoving and indignant
drumming. The whole time we were on Kapiti the Wekas

stayed with us, scuttling around like little brown gnomes, busy-bodying about, tripping us up and keeping up their incessant drumming. They were charming but exhausting companions.

At first it seemed as though Wekas were the only bird inhabitants of Kapiti, but once we had got the equipment out and the cameras and tripods set up, the other birds started to appear. The first to arrive for a quick snack at the small bird table George Fox had fitted up was a Bellbird. He hid in the trees nearby for some time before he came down to the table, but while we waited for him to show himself he entertained us with a concert of wonderful, flute-like notes, wild and liquid and beautiful. When the bird itself appeared it was rather a disappointment, looking extremely like—at first glance—a common European Greenfinch, except that the head was a deep purplish colour. After some food and a drink he perched himself on a branch just above the food table and gave us another short concert, and you felt you could forgive him his rather uninspiring appearance for the sake of the wonderful Pan pipes he could play with such elegance and ease.

The next bird to arrive gave me a considerable shock, for it was completely unlike how I had imagined it. It was a New Zealand Pigeon and it circled once round the house in fat, rather self-satisfied flight, then settled on the lawn and proceeded to feed within a few feet of me. Now for some reason I had always imagined that this pigeon would look something like an ordinary Woodpigeon or, at the most, perhaps have the subtle colouring of a Turtle Dove. But I was not prepared for this huge and brilliant bird, which seemed to be twice the size of a Woodpigeon and with a flamboyant colouring that would have done credit to one of the tropical fruit pigeons. Its head, neck and the upper part of its breast were a vivid shade of golden-green with a coppery bloom on it, a sort of patina on the feathers, while the back was a chestnut purple, again with this coppery patina. The lower half of the back, the rump and part of the tail were metallic green, while some of the tail and wing coverts were bronze-green. The tail was brown with a sort of green wash to it. To crown it all, the bird had the base half of its beak crimson and the other half yellow, while the eyelids were red. The plumage of this pigeon, as it waddled about like an over-dressed Dowager Duchess, made the green grass look positively drab.

I had hardly finished enthusing over the pigeon when a Tui arrived, and it was quite obvious from the start that here was an artist down to the wingtips. He appeared suddenly in some bushes, casual and elegant, dressed in metallic green plumage picked out here and there with a purplish sheen. Overlying the greenish feathers on the back of his neck were fine, long, hair-like feathers in white, and at his throat he wore two small powder-puffs of white feathers that looked exactly like a cravat so exquisitely tied that even Beau Brummel might have envied it. The Tui is about the size of a blackbird, but where the blackbird is plump and rather uncouth, the Tui is slender and debonair and moves with all the ease and grace of a professional dancer. Having studied us briefly, he glanced around and chose a platform for his performance. From our point of view, he could not have chosen a better spot for it was a bare, dead branch some twenty feet away from us, where he was nicely silhouetted against the pale sky. Then he gave us a quick glance to make sure we were ready, and burst into song. Now, I had heard the Tui's singing ability lauded to the skies ever since I had landed in New Zealand, but every country you go to has its own pet bird that it swears will out-sing anything in the world, so, over the years, I have learnt to take these stories with a pinch of salt. After five minutes of the Tui's song, however, I decided that the New Zealanders had not exaggerated; if anything, they had understated, for the Tui's song was one of the most varied and skilful I have ever heard. Liquid trills, babbles and croons mixed cunningly with other strange noises which sometimes sounded like harsh coughs or even sneezes. To mix this sort of noise in with its normal song and make it sound as though it *should* be there was a consummate bit of artistry.

So seduced were we by the Tui's song that we almost forgot what we had really come to Kapiti to see, until Brian reminded us. This was a flock of Kakas, one of the large New Zealand parrots, that lived in the forests but had been taught to come when called. George disappeared briefly into the bungalow and reappeared with a handful of sticky, dried dates. Then, when we had the cameras set up, he took up his position near the bird table and started to call the Kakas.

'Come on, then,' he bellowed, his voice echoing and bouncing among the forested hills, 'come on, Henry, Lucy . . . come on then, come on my pets . . . Henry . . . Lucy . . . come on, then.'

For about five minutes he called and nothing happened; then, suddenly, a speck appeared flying high and swiftly with rapid wing-beats above the dark green forest. The Kaka swooped down at the bungalow and made a perfect landing on the corrugated roof, where I could get a good view of it through my glasses. It was a very large bird with an elongated and rather slender curved beak for a parrot; the forehead was grey and the feathers surrounding the eyes started as a reddish-orange that turned to crimson underneath the eye. The back was brown, but a sort of shot silk brown with many shifting, subtle colours in it, and the feathers on the back and rump were crimson. The top half of the breast was grey, changing to crimson on the belly and underneath the tail. It attempted to walk along the ridge of the roof, in that curious waddling gait of the parrot, and once or twice its feet slipped and it had to flap its wings to keep its balance, and I saw that the underside of the wings was bright red barred with brown. It waddled cautiously along the ridge until it came to the guttering. Here its feet could find better purchase, so it shuffled sideways down the gutter until it reached a position where it could survey us all in comfort.

It gazed at us out of bright brown eyes for some minutes, unmoved by George's plaintive efforts to get it to come down. Then, obviously deciding that we might look better from a different angle, it hung upside down and peered at us this way. It stayed like this for some ten minutes and then, deciding that although eccentric-looking we must be harmless, it flew down in a tumble of crimson wings and landed on the food table. Here it strutted and danced about while George and I fed it on bits of date. While we were doing this, two other Kakas appeared out of the forest and went through identical performances, walking along the roof, examining us from all angles, and then eventually flying down to the table. One of these late-comers was a baby, and after grabbing a piece of date he flew nervously back to the roof of the bungalow and left what were obviously his parents squabbling shrilly over the sticky offerings of dates on the food table. Carried away by his enthusiasm the male even flew up and perched on my head, much to Chris's delight, but I soon found that to have a large and heavy parrot clinging to one's scalp with an extremely sharp set of claws, whilst dropping bits of semi-masticated date into one's hair at the same time, was not my idea of the ideal form of bird watching. Also, the Kakas' sharp beaks looked powerful, so I had to keep up a continuous stream of dates for fear that I might otherwise have an ear amputated. While I was keeping the male occupied, George told me the story of the Kakas.

Apparently there was a flock of seventeen birds who came down regularly to the bird table when shouted for; unfortunately, the day we were there the majority of the flock must have been over the other side of the island and so could not hear George's stentorian bellows. This Kaka tea party had started off with just two or three birds which lived in the forest near the bungalow. These soon realised that the human inhabitants of the house not only were harmless but were willing to provide them with all sorts of delicacies which they could not find in the surrounding forest, so they very soon became regular visitors. The news of this bounty soon spread along the grapevine—or whatever the bird equivalent is—and so within a very short time there were seventeen Kakas swooping down on the bungalow if any human being so much as raised his voice.

While George was telling me all this I was amused to notice that the baby, still perching precariously on the roof and lacking the courage to come down and join its parents, was flapping its wings and uttering plaintive, throaty cries. The female on the bird table, when she felt herself sufficiently gorged on dates, gathered up a couple in her beak and flew up to the roof, where she proceeded to stuff them into the eagerly gaping maw of her offspring, who wheezed asthmatically with excitement and flapped his wings so vigorously that he almost fell off the roof. Four times she repeated this performance until the baby was wearing a pensive, slightly bloated expression. By then, George's supply of dates had come to an end and the Kakas, after careful investigation to make sure that we really *were* dateless, flew off into the forest, with the baby trailing behind, still wheezing and whining like a spoilt child.

By now the light had become too dim for successful photography so we reluctantly packed up our equipment and took our leave of Kapiti. As the launch ploughed its way across the channel towards the mainland I looked back at the island, now just a black silhouette against a pale green and gold sunset. The wild birds of Kapiti were, I reflected, not so very unusual. If birds and animals anywhere in the world were left in peace and knew that they could trust the humans with whom they came in contact, the world could be full of Kapitis—in fact, with a bit of effort, the whole world could be one gigantic Kapiti, and how wonderful that would be. But that, I reflected sourly, was an idea which was never likely to materialise.

CHAPTER 2

The Three-Eyed Lizard

Yet at first sight the crew were not pleased with the view,
Which consisted of chasms and crags.

Hunting of the Snark

WE CROSSED OVER from Wellington to South Island by the
ferry, and as we were suffering the charms of this sea voyage
Brian told us that there were two things in South Island
that he particularly wanted us to see, for they were both
conservation success stories. One was the Royal Albatross
colony at Taiaroa Head and the other was the breeding ground
of the Yellow-Eyed Penguins. After this, he said, with the
fanatical Organising gleam in his eyes, we would visit the
off-shore island where lived one of the most fantastic reptiles
in the world, the Tuatara. Considered from every point of
view, this was an itinerary that would make any self-respecting naturalist's mouth water, and so we landed on South
Island and set off full of enthusiasm.

As we drove down towards the Otago peninsula and
Taiaroa Head, we soon discovered that South Island was
totally different in character from North Island, although the
difference was so subtle that it was hard to define. It seemed
to me that South Island was wilder and less inhabited, and
yet there were just as many farms and just as much cultivation
to be seen. I think it was because you were always conscious
of the great, jagged vertebrae of mountains which ran in a

chain along the whole of one side of the island; even if you couldn't actually see them, you were always conscious of their presence. For part of the way the road ran along the sea coast, and in places the scenery was very wild and attractive, with massive rollers shouldering their way in to the shore where strange, grey slabs of rock lay in sheets so that they looked like some giant's fossilised library. On some of these rocks were small groups of fur seals, either lying in clusters sunning themselves or plunging off the rocks into such a pounding maelstrom of water that you wondered how they could survive.

The Otago peninsula lies near the town of Dunedin, and at the extreme tip of it lies Taiaroa Head. We drove into Dunedin to pick up Stan Clark, who was the Warden of the Albatross Sanctuary, and then made our way out on to the peninsula, which was a fairly hefty chunk of land, hump-backed like the hull of a rowing boat and surrounded by steep cliffs. The humpback part of the peninsula was covered with long, tussocky grass, and it was here, in this rather bare, windswept area, that the Royal Albatross—probably the most spectacular of all seabirds—had decided to make its kingdom.

The story of this Albatross Sanctuary was fascinating, and Stan, a tall, quiet, gentle man, told me with pride how the Royals had been saved. Normally the Albatross family has the good sense to choose, for its breeding places, remote islands in stormy seas where they are safe from predators—including the worst one of all, man—but between 1914 and 1919 Royal Albatrosses were seen flying over the Otago peninsula and landing on Taiaroa Head, as though inspecting the site to see if it would be suitable for a Royal nursery. Then, in 1919, the first egg was found, causing great ornithological excitement, for this was the first time ever that Royal Albatross had been known to nest on the mainland of New Zealand. A

certain Doctor Richdale and the Otago branch of the Royal
Society did their utmost to protect the birds from interference
of two kinds: from the sort of people who would steal the
eggs or else stone the nest or parent birds (and the high proportion of such morons in the world is quite extraordinary),
or else the genuinely interested people who, by wandering
about all over the Head to examine the sitting birds, the eggs
and the chicks, did not realise that they were making the
Albatrosses nervous and liable to desert. Apart from the
human element there were the cats, dogs and ferrets that ate
a good proportion of the young birds, and rabbits, who, by
their very presence, both attracted the marauders and
threatened the vegetation and the soil; but in spite of all this
the first Royal Albatross chick flew from Taiaroa Head in
1938. Now the Otago Harbour Board and the Department
for Internal Affairs lent their support to the sanctuary, and the
people of Dunedin—led by the local Rotary Club—raised
£1,250, which enabled Stan to become the Warden of the
Sanctuary. It was necessary to fence off the area the birds
had chosen for their nesting sites so that no unauthorised person could have access; this, though it may seem an irritating
rule to many people who helped create the sanctuary, is a
necessary one. Gradually the numbers of pairs in the colony
have increased so that today there are twelve pairs nesting
there. With the minimum of disturbance, this colony will
increase in size, and once it is large enough and once the birds
have grown to trust man, then visitors will be able to see the
colony. But to allow large groups of people in at this juncture
might frighten the birds and destroy the good work that has
been done so patiently over the years.

Stan let us through the impressively padlocked gate and
then along a narrow pathway that meandered through the
tussocky grass along the cliff edge. Far below us the sea was

steel grey, wrinkled and crumpled by the wind, and skimming its surface we could see hosts of sea birds—gulls, skuas, various species of cormorant. Gradually the path started to wind up towards the high ground of the Head, and the tussocks of grass grew larger, but were interspersed with areas of quite short turf. Then Stan came to a standstill and pointed: to one side of the path, not many yards away, squatted what at first sight looked like a great ball of fluff. Closer inspection proved this to be a baby Albatross, squatting regally on the haphazard collection of twigs that a Royal Albatross fondly imagines to be a nest. It was about the size of a rotund turkey, covered with fine, snow-white down that showed off to advantage its great, dark eyes and banana-yellow beak. It squatted dumpily in its nest and glared at us like an indignant powder-puff. As we got closer to him, however, he started to get uneasy and, with a tremendous effort, hoisted himself on to his great, flat feet, raised his wings over his back, and started to clatter his beak at us like a castanet. We had to judge our distance very carefully when we were filming and photographing him, for if we had got too close, he would have regurgitated a stream of black, evil-smelling oil over both us and his impeccable white shirt front, for this is the baby Albatross's only means of defence.

Presently we left this baby in peace and moved further up the path, where we found another nest on a flat piece of turf under the lee of a tumble of rocks. The baby in this nest was a much more phlegmatic character than the previous one, and merely glanced at us briefly before continuing with the difficult task he had set himself for the day. The parent birds, in building the nest, had scattered a lot of twigs over quite a large area around it, and the baby was amusing himself by seeing how far he could stretch out, grab a twig and add it to the nest, without actually getting up. He had obviously been at the job for some time, for the area immediately round the nest was bare of twigs and he was having to stretch out further and further, sometimes in danger of rolling out of the nest like a down-covered football.

I lay down on the turf just out of spitting range and watched his earnest nest-building endeavours, but soon the supply of twigs ran out and, after he had shuffled round and round in the nest to make sure there were no more twigs he could reach, he squatted there and stared into the middle distance, as if meditating some grave and important matter. I found a fairly lengthy twig and, hitching myself forward cautiously, I held it out to him. For a moment he fixed me with a penetrating stare, and then he leant forward and took the twig delicately in his beak with much the same air as that of a female member of the aristocracy receiving a somewhat battered bouquet from a snotty-nosed village child. He held it in his beak for a moment and then carefully tucked it in one side of the nest that he obviously thought showed signs of dis-repair. Encouraged by his condescension I found another twig, hitched myself still closer and offered him that. He took it immediately and became quite animated. First he stuck it in one side of the nest, then he decided it did not look right there, so he pulled it out and stuck it somewhere else. After two or three tries he was satisfied and then he looked at me expectantly: obviously, repulsive though I might appear, as a twig collector I had my points. Within ten minutes he had added several more twigs to his nest and had allowed me to lie within a couple of feet of him without spitting in my eye. Within half an hour we were bosom pals and he was even allowing me to re-arrange one or two twigs for him that he had got slightly muddled with (one he had stuck under his wing by mistake). As I watched this circular, fluff-covered chick working so intently at his nest repairing, it seemed incredible that one day he would be a handsome white bird with black wings and a yellow beak, floating effortlessly over the waves on a ten-and-a-half foot wingspan. In nine years' time, when he (or was it a she?) had reached maturity, a mate would be found and they would come back to Taiaroa Head to build their nest and rear their own fluff-covered chick. Both the parents would sit on the egg and both would help in the task of caring for the baby; then, when the chick was old enough to fend for itself, they would fly off to sea, to return two years later to repeat the performance. The Royal Albatross pairs for life and the oldest one in the colony is thirty-five, but the slow rate of reaching maturity, the long incubation (eleven weeks, one of the longest of any bird), and the fact that they have only one chick every two years, means that to build up an Albatross colony is an extremely slow process and needs a lot of patience.

As we took our reluctant leave of the chicks and made our way down the path, we saw one of the parent birds, far out on the horizon, floating like a black and white cross over the grey sea, swooping and gliding on the air currents as smoothly as a stone skims on ice, with never a single wing-beat, just a gentle inclination of the body to make the best use of whatever air current happened to catch the broad wings. We stood and watched this effortless flight until the bird was so far away that it was out of range of even our binoculars, and then, saluting the chicks once more, we left the sanctuary.

Next we drove down the coast of the peninsula to a place that Stan said was one of the favourite breeding grounds for the Yellow-Eyed Penguin. This is one of the most beautiful of the penguin family and at one time was quite common along certain areas of suitable coast, but, wherever man appeared, the penguin suffered. Yellow-Eyes like to nest inland, in the forest or scrub, the nest being placed under the shelter of a log or some rocks and consisting of a comfortable platform of twigs and coarse grass. But the human beings cut down the forest and scrub to make grassland for their precious sheep, depriving the penguin in many places of its natural nesting habitat, and so it started to decline. Add to this that the farmers and other people would raid the nests, break the eggs and kill the defenceless parent birds, and you have, in miniature, the sort of thing that is happening all over the world to hundreds of harmless species of birds, mammals and reptiles. The area that Stan took us to was a large sheep farm, one of whose borders was formed by the high cliffs of the peninsula, but in this particular area there were many valleys sloping down to the beach, valleys thickly covered with just the sort of scrub that the penguins liked to nest in. The farmer (who must surely be one of the most enlightened in New Zealand) had agreed that these valleys should remain untouched so that they formed a sanctuary for the birds and had agreed too—since he was on the spot—to be acting, unpaid Warden of the area. Before this sensible and humane gesture was made the Yellow-Eye population had dropped alarmingly to only a few hundred birds; after a few years of this protection the population had crept up and now numbered a couple of thousand. Stan was a bit worried that we might not see any of the birds, since the breeding season was over and the Yellow-Eyes spent most of their time out at sea, fishing, but we made our way down one of the valleys and eventually found ourselves on a great stretch of beach, liberally sprinkled with sea-smoothed rocks draped in shawls of green seaweed. We picked our way through the boulders, keeping a sharp look-out both up the valleys and out to sea, for we had no means of knowing where the penguins would be. Half an hour passed and we had seen nothing except a few gulls and cormorants flying past, and I began to think that, for the first time in New Zealand, we were going to be unlucky in our search for something we wanted to film. Then Stan, standing up on a pinnacle of rock, suddenly pointed out to sea.

'There's one,' he said triumphantly, 'and he's swimming inshore.'

Brian and I hurriedly scrambled up the slippery slope of rock to join him.

'Ah, yes,' said Brian in a self-satisfied manner, 'he should land about fifty yards from here.'

I peered hopefully out to sea, but my eyes were no match for those of Brian and Stan, and until I used my binoculars I could not see a thing. Then all I could see was the head which, at that distance, looked like a small bundle of straw floating rapidly along the surface of the water towards the shore.

We waited patiently on the rock until the penguin reached the shallow water and waddled ashore, as Brian had predicted, some fifty yards away from where we were. He trundled up the beach with that earnest, flat-footed air that penguins adopt and, acting on Sam's advice, we let him get up to the top of the small cliff leading to the valley before trying to intercept him. When he had crossed the beach he reached the tumble of great rocks and smaller boulders that formed the small 'cliff' at the top of which the grass and bushes started and sloped gently upwards. Instead of picking his way through these rocks, as I imagined he would, he paused in front of the first one, gathered himself for the effort and then jumped on top of it, where he stood swaying in a triumphant but slightly intoxicated manner. Then he measured the distance between the rock he was standing on and the next one and leapt once again, landing on it more by good luck than good judgement. So he progressed from rock to rock in a series of wild leaps; occasionally he would mis-

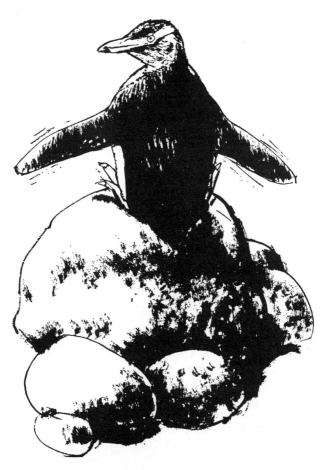

judge the distance, land on the rock, stand swaying for a moment, his wings outstretched to try and keep his balance, and would then slide gracefully down the side of the rock and out of sight. Presently he would reappear, clambering manfully up on to the rocks again, to repeat the performance. Why he chose this complicated and exhausting method of obtaining his goal I have no idea, for by picking his way between the rocks he could have obtained his objective much more quickly and in an infinitely more dignified manner. He was by now sufficiently far from the sea that, even if he did notice us, he would not have time enough to escape, so I made my way to the top of the cliff and crawled through the undergrowth on all fours until I came to the spot where I thought he would finally appear. Here I lay down in the grass and endeavoured to look as much like a piece of vegetation as possible. I had calculated that he would reach the small cliff top some twenty feet from where I was lying.

I was lying there, staring eagerly at the spot at which I thought he would appear, and making plans as to the best way to catch him so that we could take our close-up shots of him, when his head appeared over a tuft of grass some four feet away. I am not quite sure which one of us was the most surprised. The penguin glared at me in a disbelieving fashion and I gaped at him open-mouthed for, up until then, I had only seen him at a distance and I had not realised how attractive he would be. The feathers on the top of his head were bright yellow, each feather with a central black streak; a patch round his eye, which then formed a band right round the back of his head to the other eye, was a brilliant sulphur yellow; his beak was brownish with slate blue patches and his eyes were a pale lemon yellow. I lay as still as I could and hoped that he would mistake me for a rock or a bush, although I felt the chances were slight. However, the Yellow-Eye stared at me for a time, obviously suspicious, twisting his head this way and that to see if I looked any different from different angles, and at length decided that I must be some curious sort of flotsam of a harmless nature. With one final effort he hauled himself over the rim of the cliff and stood there panting, flapping his wings up and down. I could see now that his back was a pale smoke blue and his flippers were blackish, neatly rimmed with yellow, while his shirt front gleamed a pure and unsullied white, so brilliant that it would have made a detergent manufacturer burst into tears of joy. His large, rather flat feet were pinkish, armed with exceptionally large brown claws, which I supposed he needed to help him in his perambulations up and down the cliff. After he had paused long enough to gain his breath, he turned round and started to waddle up the valley with an air of determination. I rose silently to my feet, overtook him in a couple of quick steps and grabbed. I was careful to get one hand round the back of his neck, for what I had seen of his beak led me to believe that it was not put there just for ornament. As I grabbed him he twisted his head round and stared up at me in horror, at the same time uttering a startled squawk. Talking to him soothingly, I bundled his fat body under my arm and then—still keeping a firm grip on his neck—made my way down to where the others were waiting for me on the beach. After my capture had been duly admired and all the still photographs we wanted of him taken, we then hoped we would get some co-operation from him in the filming. We had the shots of him coming out of the sea and some long shots of him climbing the cliff, but what we wanted now were some close-up shots of him boulder-hopping. To our complete surprise, he behaved perfectly. We put him down on the sand within a few feet of the tumble of boulders and he started off towards them determinedly. For five minutes or so we filmed him leaping from boulder to boulder with what he obviously imagined to be a Chamois-like grace, occasionally tripping and falling on his face or toppling over backwards and disappearing into a crevice with wild flapping of flippers. When we had all the material we wanted we decided that it would be a shame—after his original laborious ascent of the cliff—that he should have to do it all over again because of us, so I picked him up and carried him a fair distance up the valley in the direction in which he had been originally heading. I put him down on the grass and he looked up at me enquiringly; I patted his bottom encouragingly and he waddled a few uncertain paces forward and then looked back again, as if wondering whether it was worth going any further if I was going to chase and catch him again, but as I remained quite still he decided that perhaps now he was safe, and disappeared into the long undergrowth at a brisk trot, tripping daintily over the grass tussocks, and soon disappeared from sight. As I watched him go I wondered how anyone could be so callous as to kill these beautiful and harmless birds, or even rob their nesting sites, but at least there was one consolation: here, on this strip of wild coast with the gentle, tree-filled valleys running up from the sea, they were safe.

We drove back into Dunedin, dropped Stan at his house, and then pointed the nose of the Land-Rover back the way we had come. Our destination was Picton, the port on the extreme tip of South Island, for it was from here that we were to take the trip out to the Brothers.

The following morning we made our way down to the jetty in Picton and found the boat that was to take us to the Brothers. She was a small, rather raffish-looking launch, with a wheelhouse the size of a matchbox. Jim, festooned with equipment like a Christmas tree, gazed at it uneasily.

'Are we going in *that*?' he asked.

'Yes. What's wrong with it? It's a dear little boat,' said Jacquie, and I saw the launch's owner wince visibly.

'But it's so small,' said Jim. 'There are no cabins.'

'We'll only be on her for a few hours. What on earth do you want cabins for?'

'You have to have *somewhere* to go if you feel sick,' said Jim in a dignified tone.

'You can be sick over the side,' said Chris callously.

'*I* like to be sick in private,' said Jim.

'Well, stick a coat over your head,' said Chris.

'Come along, come along, let's get started,' said Brian, rushing to and fro carrying things. We got the last of the equipment on and then scrambled aboard ourselves. The skipper of the launch cast off and started the engine and we set off down Queen Charlotte Sound, our dinghy bobbing and bouncing about in our wake like an excited puppy chasing its mother's tail.

The water of the Sound was as flat as a pale blue mirror, and reflected in it were the rolling, browny-green, rather desiccated-looking hills along each side. We crowded on to the tiny deck in the bows of our craft and lay basking in the thin sunshine, keeping a sharp look-out for birds. Here Brian came into his own, for his phenomenal eyesight enabled him to pick out and identify species long before we had our eyes attuned to the silky blue reflection of the water. Luckily, however, most of the bird life we saw was reasonably tame and allowed the boat to get quite close before scattering. The first and by far the most common species we saw were the Fluttering Shearwaters, small, fragile-looking birds, blackish-brown in colour with white undercarriages and ashy grey marking on the head. They freckled the water in little clusters of four or five and would let us get to within about twenty feet of them before taking off and flying along the surface of the water with a rapid, rather twisting flight, their wings flapping rapidly in the characteristic Shearwater flight that has given them their name. We were endeavouring to get some good cine shots of the Fluttering Shearwaters when Brian pointed out to me a mysterious round object floating on the surface of the water.

'Penguin!' he said succinctly.

I stared at the rounded object incredulously; it bore

absolutely no resemblance whatsoever to any bird species I had ever seen. Suddenly the ball swivelled round and I saw it had a beak attached to it. Sure enough, it was the head of a penguin, swimming along with the body completely submerged and only the head showing above the surface, like the periscope of a submarine. As the boat drew closer to it we could distinguish the body beneath the clear water and watch it as it propelled itself along with its flippers and feet. It was a species of penguin that I had always wanted to meet—the Cook Strait Blue Penguin, the smallest of this extraordinary family. Tubby little birds, they stand only sixteen inches high; their shirt fronts are an immaculate, shining, first-night white, and the rest of their plumage a beautiful deep blue, nicely set off by a neat white line down the outside of each flipper. The one we were following seemed more cautious than afraid, for he would let the boat come within twenty or thirty feet of him before suddenly submerging and zooming off like a torpedo, leaving a trail of silvery bubbles behind him. Then he would pop to the surface when he was well ahead, and float there, watching us with interest until the boat was nearly on top of him again. Presently he was joined by six or seven others, and they led us along like a guard of honour for several miles. They were enchanting little birds and the more we saw of them the more we grew to like them, although, as we were soon to learn, close proximity to them could be irritating.

After chugging down the Sound for an hour or so, we rounded a headland and ahead of us could see the mouth of the Sound. Here we would be entering the open sea of Cook Strait. We could see that the water ahead was not the smooth, pale blue water of the Sound, but a deep, rich, peacock blue, flecked and striped with foam.

'Looks as though it's going to be a bit rough,' shouted our

skipper, cheerfully. Jim, who had been lying back with his eyes closed and a beatific smile on his face, sat up in alarm and looked ahead.

'Cor, stone the crows,' he said, 'are we going out into *that*?'

'What really worries me is that if it's too rough we won't be able to land on the White Rocks *or* the Brothers,' said Brian.

'It doesn't worry me,' said Jim, 'not in the least. Let's turn back and film some more penguins.'

'Oh, it's not too bad,' said our skipper. At that moment we hit the demarcation line between the calm waters of the Sound and the boisterous waters of Cook Strait. The launch, like a skittish horse, immediately tried its best to stand on its head, and a vast quantity of spray was flung on to the deck where we were sitting. We rose in a body and struggled back to wedge ourselves in the tiny wheelhouse which at least gave us some protection.

'We're mad—stark, staring mad,' said Jim, desperately trying to keep his balance and mop seawater off the lens of his camera.

'Just a bit of a blow,' said the skipper amusedly, 'but it might make it a bit tricky getting on to the White Rocks, that's all.'

'How do we get on there?' asked Jim.

'In the dinghy,' replied the skipper.

Jim glanced out over the stern and was treated to the sight of the tiny dinghy on the end of her rope completely disappearing behind a wave.

'A bit tricky,' said Jim thoughtfully. 'That is one of the most masterly understatements I have ever heard.'

Although to anyone used to small boats this sea was nothing, to anyone who suffered acutely from seasickness it must have seemed as though we were in the middle of a typhoon.

However, I could quite see the skipper's point of view that to get on to an almost sheer rock without adequate anchorage in a sea like this *was* going to be tricky. It was not long before we caught our first glimpse of the White Rocks through the salt-encrusted windows of the wheelhouse, and I began to realise how difficult the landing might be. It reared up out of the sea like a medium-sized pyramid with a carunculated top. The upper surface of the rock was white with the droppings of generations of seabirds, and this gave it the appearance of a badly shaped and badly iced Christmas cake. The skipper edged the launch round to the seaward side of the rock, where there was a slight recess that could hardly be dignified with the term bay. Here he cut the engine down as much as possible and his second in command pulled the dinghy alongside the wallowing, rolling launch. Getting from the launch into the dinghy in that sea was quite a feat in itself, but to do it while carrying heavy but delicate equipment required the agility of a gibbon, and I was sure at one point when Jim stumbled that he would pitch headfirst into the sea and sink from sight, pulled under by the weight of the stuff he was carrying. One by one, Chris, Jim, Brian and I were ferried across and landed on a beach the size of the average dining table at the base of the rock; with the four of us and the equipment on the beach, there was little room for anything else.

As Brian explained to us, the nesting site of the King Shags was on a small, flat area on the very crest of the White Rocks, and in order to get to it we would have to scale the cliff under which we now stood. Jim glanced at the almost vertical rock face and raised his eyes to heaven. Actually, the climb was not difficult, for the wind and rain had gouged and fretted the rock face to such an extent that there were a thousand hand and footholds. What made the climb at all dangerous was the composition of the White Rocks: the whole thing was as brittle and crumbly as sponge cake and you could literally break off great chunks of it with your bare hands, so every foothold and handhold had to be tested and double checked. Also, the wind had acted like a whetstone, sharpening every projection to a razor edge, and this was an added hazard. Laboriously we climbed up the cliff, and when we reached the top and peered over, the wind hit us with such force that it almost blew both us and the equipment into the sea. We were now clinging to the summit, some hundred and fifty feet above the sea. To our right a coffin-shaped slab of stone projected out over the waves, and to our left the fretted spine of the rock ran along for some two hundred feet and then petered out into a flattish area about fifty feet by twenty, and there was the colony of King Shags. There were about twenty of them squatting on the rock among their nests, and as our heads appeared above the edge of the rock they all waddled to the edge and took off, sweeping and wheeling round us, showing on their backs as they flew two curious, circular white patches that looked like the headlights of a car. They flew round in ever increasing circles until the whole flock were mere pinpricks against the blue sky. Brian assured us that they would soon return, and so Jim, having sized up the photographic possibilities of the situation, insisted on crawling out and lying on the coffin-shaped projection to our right; this in spite of our protests, for the rock was so brittle that the whole chunk could have broken off under his weight and precipitated him a hundred and fifty feet to the sea below. This was typical of Jim: he spent most of his time trying to persuade you that he was the most arrant coward and yet, when he had a camera in his hands, he would take risks that would make your blood run cold. So we crouched there in the biting wind, endeavouring to look as much like part of the rock as possible, and waited for the King Shags to return.

While we waited, I trained my binoculars on to the nesting site and examined the nests. These were circular structures some two feet in diameter and about nine inches in height, made of a mixture of plants and seaweed cemented together with the birds' excreta, and as they are added to each year some were considerably higher than others. The White Rocks are, of course, as bare of vegetation as a billiard ball, so the birds have to fly to other nearby islands to collect their nesting material. The list of plants used in this nest building reads like something out of Lewis Carroll: taupata twigs, scurvy grass and mesembryanthemum.

The shags were a long time coming back and Brian started to get worried, for the weather was getting worse and soon we should either have to go back to the launch without filming them, or run the very real risk that the launch might have to leave us marooned on the White Rocks. The latter prospect did not enthral any of us, for a night spent on the rock would hardly appeal to even the most spartan of souls, but then we saw the shags returning, wheeling through the sky, their strange headlight markings showing up brilliantly white against the darkness of the backs. They flew lower and lower over the rock, and then one, bolder than the rest, swooped in and landed on the nesting site. Within a few minutes the rest, emboldened by his action, had joined him.

While Jim's camera was whirring away, I had plenty of time to watch the birds through my binoculars. They were about the size of a European Gannet, but with the typical upright stance of the shag and cormorant family; they had beautiful metallic bluey-green backs and white shirt fronts, and the bare skin round the base of the beak and the eye was brilliant orange and blue. They flapped and waddled among their nests, adding bits of seaweed to the structures and occasionally pinching nice bits of nesting material from their neighbours' nests, if the neighbours were not looking. In one corner of the nesting site a fully adult youngster, still in his drab, immature plumage, pursued his parent round and round the nest—mouth open, wings fluttering, and wailing peevishly for food. Eventually the mother, bored by his continuous pursuit, stopped and opened her beak to him, whereupon the baby, with a wild squawk of delight, dived in head first, his head and part of his neck disappearing down her throat. This action he accompanied with much wing flapping, so that the parent bird was hard put to it to retain her balance. It really looked as though the baby was trying to disembowel her. Eventually, when it was obvious that she had regurgitated as much as she was able to, he withdrew his head with reluctance and sat there clattering his beak and uttering tiny, self-satisfied wails and belches to himself. The parent bird, obviously relieved, wandered off, hastily swiped a piece of seaweed from somebody else's nest, and proceeded to do some running repairs to her own.

By now the wind had increased in force and far below us we could see the launch pitching and tossing as she revolved in tight circles. We had taken all the film we needed, so it seemed only prudent to get off the White Rocks while we were still able to. We found the descent infinitely more hazardous than the climb up had been, but we eventually ended up on the minute beach, scratched and breathless but intact. As we boarded the launch and headed out to sea, a small group of King Shags took off from the rock and flew over us, wheeled round and settled on the rock again. I wondered how long these wonderful seabirds could hold out against extinction: the White Rocks are one of the only two nesting places for the King Shag in the world, and the White Rocks can hardly be called a desirable residence, for each year a bit more of it is eaten away by the rapacious wind and the sea. Also, there are several different kinds of shag and cormorant in New Zealand, and some of these, the fishermen claim, do damage to the fishing, so they are allowed to shoot them in certain areas—one of the areas being in the vicinity of the White Rocks. Now the average fisherman out to shoot cormorants or shags is either not sufficient of a naturalist to distinguish between the King Shag and the other species, or else he simply does not care. As far as he is concerned, the bird is a fish eater and should therefore be shot, so the future of the King Shag is, to say the least, uncertain.

The launch chugged on for half an hour or so and then, through the spray-distorted windows of the wheelhouse, we could see two humps of rock on the horizon, rather resembling the large and small humps of a camel. I went out on deck and peered at our destination through the binoculars: the smaller of the two humps appeared to be nothing more than a desolate lump of rock, unrelieved by anything except the white frill of breakers it wore round its base; the larger of the two humps, however, appeared to have some vegetation on it, and at one end stood the tall shape of the lighthouse. These, then, were the Brothers, and it was here (depending on whether we could get ashore) that I hoped to see the reptile that rejoiced in the name of *Sphenodon punctatus*, or the Tuatara. Brian had sent a telegram to Alan Wright who, together with two companions, ran the lighthouse, asking him (a) if they would put us up for a couple of days, and (b) whether he could catch a couple of Tuataras for us. The reason for the last request was that now our time was growing short in New Zealand, and as we could only afford to spend a couple of days on the Brothers, we did not want to spend the time chasing elusive Tuataras to try and film them. In due course we had received a laconic reply saying that Alan Wright *could* put us up, would see what he could do about

Tuataras, and would Brian please put ten bob each way on a horse called High Jinks, which was due to come romping home at about a hundred to one in some race or other. Brian had been pleased with the telegram but I had felt that the frivolous tone of the whole missive boded ill for us. However, we were there now and all we could do was to wait and see what happened.

As we got nearer to the larger of the Brothers we could see that it rose sheer out of the sea, the cliffs being some two hundred feet high. On top of a flat area at the edge of the cliff crouched what appeared to be a baby crane looking, as cranes always do, like a surrealistic giraffe. The launch headed for the cliffs below the crane and we could see a group of three people standing around its base; they waved vaguely at us and we waved back.

'I suppose,' I asked Brian, 'that that crane's the way they get supplies on to the island?'

'It's the way they get everything on to the island,' said Brian.

'Everything?' asked Jim, 'What d'you mean by everything?'

'Well, if you want to get on to the island you've got to go by crane. There is a path up the cliffs, but you could never land on the rocks in this sort of weather. No, they'll lower the net down in a minute and have you up there in a jiffy.'

'D'you mean to say they're thinking of hauling us up that cliff in a *net?*' asked Jim.

'Yes,' said Brian.

Just at that moment the skipper of the launch cut the engines down, and we drifted under the cliff, rising and falling on the blue-green swell and watching the breakers cream and suck at the jagged cliff some twenty-five feet away. The nose of the crane appeared high above, and from it dangled —at the end of an extremely fragile-looking hawser—something closely resembling a gigantic pig net. The crane uttered a series of clankings, groans and shrieks that were quite audible, even above the noise of the wind and the sea, and the pig net started to descend. Jim gave me a mute look of anguish and I must say that I sympathised with him. I have no head for heights at all and I did not relish, any more than he did, being hauled up that cliff in a pig net slung on the end of a crane that, from the sound of it, was a very frail octogenarian who had been without the benefit of oil for a considerable number of years. Chris, wrapped up in his duffle coat and looking more like a disgruntled Duke of Wellington than ever, started Organising with the same fanatical gleam in his eye that Brian always had in similar situations.

'Now I want you to go up first, Jim, and get the camera set up by the crane so that you can film Gerry and Jacquie as they land,' he said. 'I'll go up next and get shots of the launch from the net, and then Gerry and Jacquie will follow with the rest of the equipment. Okay?'

'No,' said Jim. 'Why should I have to go first? Supposing the thing breaks just as I get to the top? Have you seen the rocks down here?'

'Well, if it breaks we'll know it's unsafe and go back to Picton,' said Jacquie sweetly.

Jim gave her a withering look as he reluctantly climbed into the pig net, which had by now landed on the tiny deck of the launch. The skipper waved his hand, there was a most terrifying screech of tortured metal, and Jim, clinging desperately to the mesh of the pig net, rose slowly and majestically into the air, whirling slowly round and round.

'I wonder if he gets net-sick as well as sea-sick?' said Jacquie.

'Sure to,' said Chris callously. 'To the best of my knowledge he gets sea-sick, train-sick, car-sick, plane-sick and home-sick, so I can't see him escaping being net-sick as well.'

Jim was now about halfway up, still twisting round and round, his white face peering down at us from between the meshes of the net.

'We're all *mad*,' we heard him yell above the sound of the sea and the infernal noise the crane was making. He was still yelling presumably insulting remarks at us when the net disappeared over the edge of the cliff. After a pause it reappeared again and was lowered to the deck, where Chris stepped stoically into it. He stuck his nose and the lens of the camera through the mesh of the net and started to film the moment he was lifted from the deck. Higher and higher he rose, still filming, and then suddenly, when he was poised halfway between the launch and the top of the cliff, the net came to a sudden halt. We watched anxiously but nothing happened for about five minutes, except that Chris continued to go round and round in ever diminishing circles.

'What d'you think has happened?' asked Jacquie.

'I don't know. Perhaps Jim's jammed the crane to get his own back on Chris.'

Just as I said this the crane started up again and Chris continued his majestic flight through the air and disappeared over the cliff edge. We discovered later that Jim had set up his camera and tripod in such a position that Alan Wright could not swing the crane in, but Alan was under the impression that Jim had to be in that particular position, so he kept Chris dangling in mid-air. It was only when he saw Jim leave the camera, find a convenient rock and, squatting on it, take out a bar of chocolate and start to eat it, that he realised that he had been keeping Chris dangling like a pantomime fairy to no good purpose, so the camera and tripod were removed and Chris was swung in, demanding vociferously to know why he had been kept suspended in mid-air for so long.

The net was sent down once again, loaded up with our gear, and Jacquie and I reluctantly took our seats.

'I am not going to like this a bit,' said Jacquie with conviction.

'Well, if you get scared just close your eyes.'

'It's not the height so much,' she said, glancing upwards, 'it's the strength of that hawser that worries me.'

'Oh, I wouldn't worry about *that*,' I said cheerfully. 'I expect it's been carrying loads like this for years.'

'That's exactly what I mean,' she said grimly.

'Well, it's too late now,' I said philosophically, as the crane started its banshee-like screech and we zoomed up from the deck of the launch at the speed of an express lift. The wide mesh of the net gave you the unpleasant impression that you had been rocketed into the air without any support at all, and as you revolved round and round you could see the waves breaking on the jagged rocks below. The launch now looked like a toy and, glancing up, the top of the cliff appeared to be a good deal higher than Everest, but at last we reached the cliff edge and were swung in and dumped unceremoniously on the ground.

As we disentangled ourselves from the net and equipment, a stocky man who had been operating the crane came forward and shook hands. He had a freckled face, vivid blue eyes and bright red hair.

'I'm Alan Wright,' he said. 'Pleased to meet you.'

'There were moments,' I said, glancing at the crane, 'when I began to wonder if we should ever meet.'

'Oh, she's all right,' said Alan, laughing, 'she just maithers a bit when she's got a load on, that's all.'

We got the equipment up the final slope to the lighthouse on a sort of elongated trolley, drawn up the hillside by a cable and winch. The others decided to walk up but I thought it would be fun to ride up on the trolley and so I perched myself on the camera gear. We were halfway up when I glanced back and suddenly realised that—potentially speaking—this was every bit as dangerous as the trip in the net, for if the hawser that was hauling the truck broke, the truck, weighted down with equipment and myself, would run backwards down the rails and shoot off the edge of the cliff like a rocket. I was glad when we ground to a halt by the lighthouse.

When we had got the gear safely installed in the one wooden hut which we would all have to share as bedroom and work-shop, I turned to Alan eagerly.

'Tell me,' I said, 'did you manage to get a Tuatara for us?'

'Oh, aye,' he said casually, 'that's all right.'

'Wonderful,' I said enthusiastically. 'Can I see it?'

Alan gave me an amused look.

'Aye,' he said. 'Come with me.'

He led Jacquie, Chris and myself to a small shed that stood not far from the hut we were to occupy, unlocked the door and threw it open; we all peered inside.

I have, at one time and another, had many zoological surprises, but, offhand, I can never remember being quite so taken aback as when I peered into that tiny shed on the Brothers. Instead of the one Tuatara I had expected, the whole floor was—quite literally—covered with them. They ranged from great-grandfathers some two feet long to babies measuring some six inches. Alan, glancing at my face, misinterpreted my expression of disbelieving delight for one of horror.

'I hope I haven't got too many,' he said anxiously. 'Only you didn't say what size you wanted or how many, so I thought I'd better catch you a fair selection.'

'My dear fellow,' I said in a hushed whisper, 'you couldn't have done anything to please me more. There was I, thinking we might be lucky if we just saw *one* Tuatara, and here you provide me with a positive sea of them. It's incredible. Did they take you long to catch?'

'Oh, no,' said Alan, 'I got this lot last night. I left it until the last minute because I didn't want to keep them shut up too long. But I think there'll be enough for your film, won't there?'

'How many have you got in there?' asked Chris.

'About thirty,' said Alan.

'Yes . . . well, I think we can just about scrape through with a mere thirty,' said Chris with magnificent condescension.

We returned to the lighthouse in a jubilant frame of mind and had an excellent lunch. Then we went back to the shed full of Tuataras and started to choose our stars. Crouching there in the gloom, surrounded by an interested audience of Tuataras, was a fascinating experience. All the young ones were a uniform chocolate brown, a protective coloration which they maintain until they are fully grown, but it was the coloration of the adults that amazed me. Previously the Tuataras I had seen had been unfortunate individuals incarcerated in Reptile Houses in various zoos, where the temperature was kept at a constant eighty or eighty-five degrees —a temperature which is not only totally unsuitable for the unfortunate creature, but which makes it turn a dirty brown out of sheer misery. But these wild-caught adult specimens

were how a Tuatara should look, and I thought they looked beautiful. The ground colour of the skin is a sort of greenish-brown, heavily flecked with sage green and sulphur-yellow spots and streaks; both male and female develop crests down their backs, but in the male the crest is larger and more prominent. The crests consist of little triangular bits of white skin of the consistency of thickish paper, that run down from the back of the head to the base of the tail. The tail itself is decorated with a series of hard spikes of the same shape, but whereas the spikes on the tail are the same colour as the tail, the crest along the back is so white it looks as though it is been freshly laundered. The males had massive, regal looking heads and huge dark eyes, so large that they resembled the eyes of an owl more than anything. After a lot of deliberation we chose one magnificent male, one young one, and a rather pert-looking and well-marked female. The rest of the horde we left carefully locked up in the hut: firstly because we could not release them until nightfall, and secondly, should one of our 'stars' escape during the course of the filming, we had a hut full of doubles to fall back on. But we had no difficulty like this, for every Tuatara behaved perfectly in front of the cameras and did exactly what we wanted.

Now, although to the uninitiated eye the Tuatara looks like nothing more nor less than a rather large and majestic lizard, one of the reasons that it makes naturalists like myself foam at the mouth with enthusiasm is that it is not a lizard at all. It is, in fact, so unlike the lizards in its structure that a special new order had to be created for it when it was discovered, an order called the *Rhynchocephalia*, which simply means 'beak head'. Not only did it have the distinction of having a special order created for it, but it was soon discovered that the Tuatara is a genuine, living, breathing prehistoric monster. It is the last survivor of a once widely spread group that was found in Asia, Africa, North America and even Europe. Most of the skeletons that have been found date from the Triassic period of some two hundred million years ago, and they show how alike the 'beak heads' of those days were to the present-day Tuatara; to have come down through all those years unchanged surely makes the Tuatara the conservative to end all conservatives. The other thing about this lovely animal that has captured the imagination is the fact that it has a third 'eye'—the pineal eye—situated on top of the head midway between the two real eyes, and a lot of unnecessary fuss has been made over this, for Tuataras are not unique in having a pineal eye; several kinds of lizard and some other animals have it as well. The young Tuatara, when it is hatched, has a curious 'beak' on the end of its nose (for tearing its way out of the parchment-like shell) and the pineal eye is clearly visible on top of the head. It is an uncovered spot with scales round it, radiating like the petals of a flower. This eye gradually becomes overgrown with scales and in the adult specimens it is impossible to see it. Many experiments to see whether the eye could, in fact, be of any use to the Tuatara have been tried: beams of various wavelengths have been trained on it and experiments to see whether the eye is possibly receptive to heat have all proved negative in their results. So the Tuatara just ambles through life with its three eyes, a puzzle to biologists and a joy to those naturalists who are fortunate enough to see it. At one time these creatures were found on the mainland of New Zealand, but they have long since been exterminated there, and now they only survive in limited numbers on a few islands (like the Brothers) scattered around the coast, where they—quite rightly—enjoy full protection from the New Zealand Government.

By the time we had finished filming it was sunset, and we suddenly became aware that the Brothers were not just semibarren lumps of rock populated entirely by lighthouse keepers and Tuataras. Fairy Penguins appeared in small groups and hopped their way up the rocks towards their nest burrows, pausing every now and then to throw back their heads and utter a loud, braying cry reminiscent of a small but extremely enthusiastic donkey. Then the Fairy Prions—delicate little swallow-like petrels—started to arrive. It is with the Fairy Prions that the Tuataras have worked out an amicable housing arrangement: the Prion digs a burrow for the reception of its eggs and the Tuataras move in and live with the Prions in what appears to be perfect harmony. This is principally because the Prions are out at sea, fishing, during most of the day, and so only really make use of the burrow at night—at least when they are not incubating. The Tuataras, on the other hand, come out at night in their hunt for beetles, crickets and other provender, so, as the day shift of Prions is winging its way back in the evening light, the Tuatara night shift is just leaving. It seems an admirable but curious relationship; the Tuataras are perfectly capable of digging their own burrows (and in many cases do), but the Prions seem to offer no objection to the Tuataras invading their nests. Whether the Tuataras are ever ungrateful enough to eat the eggs or young of the Prions is a moot point, but it would not be altogether surprising, for reptiles, by and large, have little conscience.

As the sun touched the horizon the Fairy Penguins started to come ashore in droves, and the Prions glided in like pale ghosts to settle among the low undergrowth and then shuffle awkwardly, in a swift-like manner, down their nesting burrows. As soon as they had disappeared underground they would start talking to each other in a series of loud, purring grunts, squeaks and pigeon-like cooings. As the nest burrows were fairly close together, one could hear twenty or thirty conversations going on at the same time and this, combined with the braying of the penguins, made the whole island literally shake. The nearer ones were, of course, the loudest, but by attuning your ear you discovered that the whole island was vibrating like a gigantic harp with this constant underground chorus.

At length the sun dipped below the sea, the sky turned blood red and then faded rapidly into darkness full of stars, and the yellow, vigilant beam of the lighthouse started to revolve slowly round and round. Presently, full of food, tired, but contented with our day's work, we picked our way down to our hut. While the others were sorting out who was going to sleep where, I took the torch and walked along the cliff edge. The Prions and Penguins were still calling with undiminished enthusiasm and then suddenly, in my torch beam, I saw a Tuatara. He was a huge male, his white frill standing up stiffly along his back, his heavy head raised as he gazed at me with his enormous eyes. After having spotted him I switched off the torch, for the moonlight was quite bright enough for me to watch him. He remained stationary for a few minutes and then started to walk very slowly, and with great dignity, through the undergrowth. All around me the ground shook with the twittering, braying, squeaking and snoring of the birds and the Tuatara strolled majestically through his moonlit kingdom like a dragon. Presently he paused again, looking at me haughtily—but the effect was spoilt, for nature has designed his mouth in a half smile—and then disappeared into the undergrowth.

I wandered sleepily back to the hut and found all the others curled up in their camp beds.

'Ah!' said Jim, poking his head out from what appeared to be a pile of some twenty blankets, 'you're interested in birds, aren't you, Gerry? Well, you'll be delighted to know that there are a couple of penguins who've got a semi-detached right under the floor of this hut.'

He had hardly finished speaking before the most raucous braying started up immediately beneath my feet. It was so loud it made speech impossible and, if we had not been so tired, it would have made sleep impossible, for the penguins sang part songs at five-minute intervals throughout the night, but, I reflected as I jammed a pillow over my head, it had been worth it just to see that one Tuatara moving with such superb nonchalance through the undergrowth of this, his own island.

CHAPTER 3

The Bird That Vanished

But the valley grew narrow and narrower still
And the evening got darker and colder.

Hunting of the Snark

IN 1948 A DISCOVERY was made in New Zealand that
shook the ornithological world out of its usual comatose condition in an incredible manner—no less than the discovery (or
re-discovery) of a bird that had vanished, a bird that had, for
the last fifty years, been believed to be extinct. It was, to give
it its full title, the Notornis or Takahe (*Notornis mantelli*),
and the whole history of this bird is one of the most fascinating
in the annals of ornithology.

The first Takahe was discovered in 1850, and excited even
the staid naturalists of those days. The bird had been known
to the Maoris from both North and South Islands, but in
North Island it was only known from fossil remains. In South
Island, the Maoris said, the Takahe had been common,
particularly around the shore of Te Anau and Manapouri, two
large glacial lakes. It was so common, in fact, that the Maoris
used to organise annual hunts during the winter, when the
snows up in the mountains drove the birds down to lower
levels in search of food, but by the time the Europeans came
to the area, only fossil remains could be found. Then, in
1849, the first live one was caught on Resolution Island in
Dusky Sound by a party of sealers, who did what human

beings usually do in these circumstances: they ate it. Two years later another Takahe was discovered and presumably suffered the same fate, but fortunately the skins of both these birds were obtained by a gentleman called Mantell, who sent them to the Natural History Museum in London. For twenty-eight years after this the Takahe vanished again, as mysteriously as it had reappeared, then, in 1879, another specimen was caught near Lake Te Anau, and in 1898 yet another was caught by a dog in the same vicinity. Now it seemed as through the Takahe was really extinct, that it had followed in the footsteps of that other famous flightless bird, the Dodo, for fifty years passed and there was no sign of it at all.

But there was a Dr. G. B. Orbell who did not believe that the Takahe had suffered the fate of the Dodo, and in 1948 he set out on an expedition to see if he could find it. The place he chose was an old glacial valley which lay high up in the mountains on the western shores of Lake Te Anau. His expedition was not a success for, apart from seeing some ill-defined footprints and hearing some unusual bird calls, he found no proof that the Takahe was still in existence. Nothing daunted, he went back to the valley seven months later, and there he found a small breeding colony of the elusive bird. This is the sort of discovery that every naturalist dreams of making, but only one in a million achieves, and so I can under-stand and envy the delight which Dr. Orbell must have felt when he caught his first glimpse of a real, live Takahe. The day after his discovery, of course, the reappearance of the Takahe was headline news all over the world, and the New Zealand Government, fearing a sudden influx of sightseers, ornithologists and other fellow travellers into this tiny valley —thus disturbing the colony—stepped in with commendable promptitude and immediately declared the whole area a vast sanctuary, making it out of bounds to anyone who was not an accredited scientist or naturalist, and even their visits were under Government and Wildlife Department supervision. So the Takahe (numbering, as far as could be judged, between thirty and fifty birds) was secure in its own sanctuary at last, a sanctuary measuring some seven hundred square miles.

Shortly after we had arrived in Wellington I had met Gordon Williams, who, at the time the Takahe was re-discovered, was a biologist attached to the New Zealand Wildlife Service. He told me about the second part of the Takahe story, which was, if anything, even more remarkable than the first.

The birds in their remote valley were certainly anything but safe, in spite of the fact that the whole area had been designated a sanctuary and no unauthorised person was let in. To begin with, their numbers were minute and it was quite possible for a sudden influx of the introduced stoat and weasel to wipe them out, or for a similar influx of introduced deer or opossums to do much the same thing by their damage to the trees, thus altering the whole habitat of the bird. So, once again, one of New Zealand's native birds was being threatened by introduced animals. It was obviously impos-sible to patrol the valley to make sure that predators, deer and opossums did not get into it, so there was only one thing to do to ensure the safety of the Takahe, and that was to try to establish a breeding colony of them in captivity; but this was not quite so easy as it appeared on the surface. First, a site for the experiment had to be chosen which closely resembled the Takahe Valley; then public opinion had to be weaned on to the side of the experimenters, for a lot of well-meaning people—not fully understanding the ramifications of the problems and the dangers that faced the newly re-discovered birds—were against 'putting them in cages'. The first problem was solved by finding a very suitable area up at Mount Bruce, some 80 miles from Wellington, and public opinion was at last persuaded that the whole scheme was for the good of the birds. So Operation Takahe came into being.

Now, as Gordon Williams explained, came the hardest part of all. In those days the only way to get into and out of the valley was to climb from the shores of Lake Te Anau up the steep, thickly forested slopes over extremely difficult terrain until you reached the narrow gorge entering the valley, two thousand five hundred feet above. This was difficult enough (as previous expeditions had found out) even if you were just going up there to film or collect scientific data; but to climb up there, collect live Takahe and bring them down again, was a feat that would make even the most hardened animal collector blanch. It was obvious that these difficulties ruled out the capture and transportation of fully adult birds, for everything taken up into or brought down out of the valley had to be transported by pack, and it was felt that the adult birds would not survive the journey; therefore, the only thing to do was to get chicks. Now this decision in itself brought up a whole host of new problems; firstly the chicks would have to have a foster-mother and it seemed that bantams, the time-honoured domestic breed of fowl for this job, were the ideal choice. But even the most phlegmatic of bantams was not going to take kindly to suddenly having a lot of Takahe chicks shoved under her, and being told to keep them warm. So the answer was to get Takahe eggs and put them under bantams, but then, as somebody pointed out, even the most well-behaved bantam, brimming over with mother love, could hardly be expected to sit tight on the eggs while being bumped and jolted all the way up to and down from Takahe Valley. Gloom and despair settled over the instigators of Operation Takahe and it seemed as if it really was going to be impossible to get any of the birds out of the valley to safety. Then somebody (I suspect Williams himself, for he was so desperately keen on the project) suggested that the bantams be 'brain-washed'—that is to say, that a series of bantams be taught to sit tight on a nest of eggs no matter *what* the circumstances were. It was a long shot but well worth trying, and now began a careful selection of bantams. Out of a hundred or so, a handful were chosen either for their dim-wittedness or their basically phlegmatic characters, and these birds had to undergo what was, to all intents and purposes, a sort of avian assault course. They each had a clutch of chicken eggs to sit on in a cardboard box, and once they were sitting firmly they were then subjected to every form of shock that they might have to cope with on their trip to and from the valley. The boxes were jolted about, they were dropped, they were driven in cars over bumpy roads, taken in trains, speedboats and aeroplanes. Gradually the bantams of weaker moral fibre started to crack, and desert their eggs, so that at the end of the experiment only three were left. Of these, one was chosen for the simple reason that, sitting on her eggs in a cardboard box, she had been placed on top of a car and a low branch had swept box, bantam and eggs straight off the roof—a piece of basic training that had not been included in the curriculum. The box, after rolling over and over for several yards, came to a halt the wrong way up, but when it was opened they found the bantam still sitting on her eggs with grim determination— and not one of the eggs was broken, for presumably they had been cushioned against the shock by her body. So this dutiful bantam was chosen for the task of being the most important member of the Operation Takahe expedition.

It must have been a nerve-racking trip for the members

of the team. Firstly, they had no means of knowing that a bantam who had behaved so beautifully down below was going to behave in the same way up in the valley, and they all knew that if they failed in their mission there would be such a sentimental public outcry that their chances of having a second attempt would be nil. To their infinite relief and credit, however, the whole thing went off without a hitch. The Takahe eggs were obtained, the bantam sat like a rock, and after giving a day or so to make sure, they started down the hazardous, slippery mountainside towards Lake Te Anau. Once they reached the shores of the lake there was a speedboat waiting to rush their precious cargo to the nearest road; here the bantam and eggs were put in a car and dashed down to Picton, there to be loaded on to a 'plane that flew them to Wellington; then another car ride, and at last the faithful bantam and her eggs were safely installed in the sanctuary at Mount Bruce. After this epic and nerve-racking trip, all the team could do was sit back and wait for the eggs to hatch, while offering up prayers that they would be fertile. In due course, however, two chicks hatched, and the team and the bantam began to look rather smug about the whole business. At last, they felt, they had achieved success. But now a new obstacle reared its ugly head. The bantam foster-mother, of course, treated the Takahe chicks exactly as if they were her own. She led them about, scratching up the leafmould vigorously and pecking at whatever tit-bits appeared, fondly imagining that the baby Takahes—like bantam chicks— would learn by her example, but the Takahes were *not* bantam chicks and followed their foster-mother about in a bewildered fashion, piping for food but unable to learn the bantam method of feeding. It was obvious that the female Takahe *feeds* her babies, and does not show them *how* to feed for themselves as the chicken does. Now the problem of feeding them was in itself a task, for it was found that baby Takahes do not gape at the mother as normal birds would do; the food is offered in the mother's beak and the babies take it from there in a sideways manner. At length a satisfactory method was worked out: the Takahe chicks were fed on blow flies and similar delicacies impaled on the end of a pencil. With this method of food intake and with the bantam to supply them with mother love and warmth at night, they grew and throve.

Now, quite apart from the rarity of the bird, this story alone would have made us want to try to see a live Takahe in its natural surroundings, so the moment we had arrived in Wellington I had applied for permission for us to go into the valley, accompanied, of course, by Brian to make sure we did not pinch any eggs or smuggle a couple of birds out under our coats. At last, to my delight, permission was granted and we set off for Lake Te Anau. As I say, in the old days the only way into the valley was to walk, but now you can do it in comparative comfort. A tiny 'plane takes you from Te Anau, flies you up the two thousand-odd feet to the valley and lands you on the small lake that covers most of the valley floor. Brian had organised the 'plane for us but we had twenty-four hours to wait, so we stayed in a palatial hotel on the shores of Te Anau—which looked like a very large and benign Scottish loch—and luxuriated in wonderfully cooked food, excellent wines and first rate service and accommodation. The average New Zealand hotel is so appalling that we appreciated this Government-run hostelry even more than we would have done otherwise.

'Make the most of this,' said Brian as I was arguing with the head waiter as to what precise shade of red I wanted my Châteaubriand, 'it's going to be really rugged when we get up into the valley.'

Warned by this, I ordered three bottles of wine instead of two.

The following morning there were two things that did not raise our spirits. Firstly, we heard that there was a small party of deer hunters occupying the hut in Takahe Valley and so there would not be room for Jacquie to come with us, and secondly, it seemed doubtful if we should be able to get off ourselves, for black clouds appeared in the sky over Te Anau and the visibility was totally unsuitable for flying in that sort of terrain. All morning we paced the shores of the lake, cursing the weather. By lunchtime it had lifted slightly, but still did not look at all hopeful. Then Brian—who had been keeping in constant touch with the float 'plane base by 'phone —appeared with a self-satisfied grin on his face.

'Come on,' he said. 'Equipment down to the landing stage. They'll be picking us up in about half an hour.'

'Wonderful!' said Chris, 'but is the weather O.K. for flying?'

'Not really,' said Brian carelessly, 'but they say better to go now and chance it than wait and have it close down on us so much that we can't get into the valley. The pilot thinks we should just about do it.'

'Quite delightful,' said Jim to Jacquie enthusiastically. 'Aren't you sorry you're not coming, my dear—zooming up into all that cloud, looking for a valley you won't be able to see, and then when you get there, looking for a bird that you won't be able to see as well? It's been just one long series of thrills, this trip has. Wouldn't have missed it for the world.'

We got the equipment down to the jetty and it was there that Brian explained that the float 'plane, being minute, could only take two passengers as well as the pilot.

'Well,' said Chris, 'I want you to go first, Jim, with the equipment . . .'

'Why is it always *me*?' demanded Jim indignantly. 'Aren't there any other volunteers around here?'

'Get as much film as you can of flying into the valley,' continued Chris, ignoring Jim's indignation, 'and then get set up and get shots of the 'plane coming in with the rest of us.'

'What happens if they dump me up there and then can't get back?' asked Jim. 'Have you thought of that? I'd be stuck up there in a deserted valley full of ferocious birds . . . no food . . . no companionship . . . and then in about ten years you come strolling up there, I suppose, and find my whitened bones stretched out in the mist . . . that's old Jim, you'll say . . . nice enough chap in his way . . . better send a postcard to his wife. Ruddy unfeeling lot.'

'Never mind, Jim,' said Jacquie consolingly. 'If you're going ahead with the supplies, you'll have Gerry's bottles of Scotch.'

'Ah!' said Jim, brightening, 'I don't mind waiting a bit up there if I've got something to *eat*—that's different.'

Presently a rather peevish humming made itself heard and soon the float 'plane appeared, zooming towards us, looking and sounding rather like an infuriated dragonfly. It touched down neatly on the lake, turned and then came drifting up along the landing stage. We loaded the equipment while Jim asked the pilot which one of the Wright brothers *he* was, and did he think that the flying machine would ever take the place of the horse. At length we bundled Jim, still protesting, into the 'plane and watched it skim across the surface of the lake and then rise into the air, leaving a trail of white foam and tiny ripples behind it. In half an hour the 'plane was back, and this time it was Chris's turn to go, taking the rest of the film gear with him. The pilot said that conditions in the valley were perfectly all right for landing and take-off, but that the weather was closing in rapidly and we would have to get a move on. Chris flew off to join Jim, and Brian and I paced the landing stage and peered anxiously at the dark clouds that appeared to be getting thicker and blacker with each passing second. At last the 'plane returned, Brian and I clambered hurriedly into it, and we were soon shooting away across the lake.

Te Anau is a long lake and for some considerable time we flew along over the water, watching the steep, thickly forested mountains on either side of us. The forest was mainly composed of beech, which had a dark green leaf, so the towering mountains looked rather gloomy and sinister. Then the pilot banked the 'plane and tucked it in closer to the mountainside, which now looked twice as gloomy and twice as steep. I have the normal person's reactions to flying; that is to say, I am always convinced either that the pilot is going to die of heart failure at a crucial moment or that both wings are going to drop off when one is taking off or landing or halfway there—this, of course, in a big 'plane. In a small 'plane I feel fairly safe: it's like the difference between riding in a high-powered car and on a bicycle. If you fall off a bicycle you think you won't be hurt and so I always get the ridiculous but comforting feeling that to crash in a small 'plane would be something you would scarcely notice, except for a few small bruises. However, our pilot now started to fly the 'plane closer and closer to the towering hillside and I began to wonder if crashing in a small 'plane *was* quite as painless as I had always thought. Then, quite suddenly, the thing that I had dreaded for years happened: the pilot appeared to go mad at the controls. He banked sharply and then started to fly straight at the mountainside. At first I thought he was merely going to fly up and over them, but he kept heading for them determinedly. By now we could see the tops of the individual trees quite clearly, and they were approaching at an alarming speed. Just as I had accepted death as the inevitable result of the pilot's manoeuvres, and the trees were only a few hundred feet away, a narrow crack (it can be dignified with no other term) appeared in the mountainside and into this we zoomed. This crack was the gorge that led into Takahe Valley and through which the lake drained down into Te Anau far below. The gorge had high, waterworn cliffs on each side, thickly covered with beech, and it was just—but only just—wide enough to take the 'plane. At one point the trees were so close to our wingtips that I swear you could have leant out and gathered a bunch of leaves. Mercifully, the gorge was not very long and within half a minute we emerged, unscathed, and there ahead of us lay Takahe Valley.

The valley is some three miles long, somewhat oval in shape, surrounded by steep hillsides thickly covered with beech. The floor of the valley is astonishingly flat and the greater part of it is covered by the calm and shallow waters of Lake Orbell. The lake, of course, lay at the end nearest to the gorge up which we had flown, but at the other end of the valley the flat ground was covered with great meadows of snow grass. As we flew over the lake the view was breathtakingly beautiful: in the distance, against a dark and stormy sky, we could see the higher peaks of the Murchison mountains, each wearing a jagged crown of snow; the mountainsides that sloped into the valley were this sombre dark green, relieved here and there with patches of paler, sage green; the lake was silver and looked as though it had been varnished, and the meadows of snow grass were golden and bright green in the fitful sunshine that kept trying to break through the dark skies. We had to fly down the full length of the valley and then bank and turn to come in to land, for this was the only way you could get down to the lake. Just as the 'plane was dropping lower and lower and the silver waters of the lake were coming rushing up to meet us, the pilot, in a laconic manner, obviously thinking that the information would be of particular interest to me at this juncture, told me that the lake was about twelve hundred yards long—just long enough, in fact (provided you did not misjudge in any way), to land the 'plane on. A slight miscalculation and you would go gliding gracefully off the end of the lake and into the gorge we had just flown up. I could see what he meant, for we touched down and raced along the water, leaving an ever widening isosceles triangle of silver ripples behind us, and eventually came to a halt with a hundred feet or so to spare at the other end of the lake. The pilot switched off the engine and grinned over his shoulder at us.

'Well, here you are,' he said, 'Takahe Valley.'

He opened the door of the 'plane and the thing that struck me immediately was the complete and utter silence. If it had not been for the very faint lapping of the water around the floats of the 'plane you would have imagined that you had been struck deaf. In fact, so acute was the silence that I swallowed hard several times, thinking that the altitude had affected my ears. Two hundred feet away, on the banks of the lake, Jim was filming our arrival and we could hear the noise of his camera as clearly as if he had been standing next to us. This silence had an extraordinary effect on one: we instinctively lowered our voices, and as we started to unload the gear every slight sound we made seemed magnified out of all proportion. The only way to get the gear ashore was to take off our shoes and socks, roll up our trousers and hump the stuff on our backs. Stepping out of the 'plane into eighteen inches of lake water was an experience I prefer to forget; I had never realised that water could be so cold without actually turning into ice. Brian and I made two trips out to the 'plane and back before we got the gear landed, and by then my legs were so numb with cold from the knees downwards that I felt as though they had been amputated. Also I had dropped one of my shoes in the lake, which had not improved my temper. Chris, standing behind Jim and the camera, wore his dispeptic Llama look.

'Er—Gerry?' he called. 'I wonder if you'd mind just doing that once more. I wasn't satisfied with the angle of the shot.'

I glared at him with chattering teeth.

'Oh, no, I don't mind a bit,' I said sarcastically, 'my dear fellow—anything for art. You wouldn't like me to take all my clothes off and swim across the lake, would you? You've only to say the word. They say with all these new drugs pneumonia's easy to cure nowadays.'

'Do it a bit slower this time,' said Jim, grinning. 'You know, as if you're really enjoying it.'

I made a rude gesture at them and Brian and I picked up our things and trudged back to the 'plane. Eventually Chris was satisfied and we were allowed to climb out of the lake. The pilot gave us a final wave, slammed the door of the 'plane shut, taxied down to the other end of the lake and then roared towards us. He flew about seventy feet over our heads and then vanished into the gorge; gradually the sound of his engine became fainter and then, blanketed by the trees, disappeared altogether and the silence enveloped us once more: suddenly the valley seemed very lonely and remote.

Just around the other side of the lake from where we stood with the piled equipment we saw a small, corrugated hut, about the size of the average garden toolshed, standing at a point where the treeline ended and the snow grass rim of the lake began.

'What's that?' enquired Jim with interest.

'That's the hut,' said Brian.

'What, you mean the place we've got to live in?' asked Jim incredulously. 'But it's not big enough for one person, let alone four.'

'There'll be seven of us in it tonight,' said Brian. 'Don't forget the deer hunters.'

'Yes, where are they, by the way?' I asked, for the hut had all the appearance of being deserted, and the long tin chimney-stack (that looked as though it had been borrowed from one of the very early steam engines) was innocent of even the faintest wisp of smoke.

'Oh, they'll be out in the hills somewhere,' said Brian. 'They'll be back this evening, I expect.'

The hut, when we finally got to it, turned out to be a structure approximately eight feet wide by twelve feet long. At one end were two wooden bunks that looked as though they had been filched from one of the lesser known and more repulsive concentration camps. In one side of the hut was a largish plate-glass window, an astonishing refinement that gave you a magnificent view down the full length of the valley, and at the opposite end from the bunks was a fireplace. It seemed to us, at first sight, that by the time we had got all the equipment inside we would all have to sleep outside, including the deer hunters. However, after much arguing and sweating, we managed to get all the equipment stacked into the hut and leave the bunks and a medium-sized area of floor space free. But for seven people to sleep in there was obviously going to be an extremely tight squeeze, to say the very least. The hunters had left a note pinned to the table, welcoming us and saying that they had left firewood and water ready, and for this we were extremely grateful. So while Jim and Chris went over the camera and recording gear, Brian and I hung our various wet garments on an improvised washing line in the fireplace, lit the fire and put the kettle on for some tea.

The sky had grown steadily blacker and the valley darker, with faint shreds of mist floating across the surface of the lake. We lit the lamps and in the soft, yellow glow of their light we set about making our evening meal. Presently we could hear voices and they sounded as if their owners were just outside the hut but, venturing out into the gloom, we could dimly see three figures making their way along the edge of the lake some quarter of a mile away. We shouted greetings to one another, then went in and put on the kettle for the deer hunters and within fifteen minutes they had joined us.

It is always wrong to say that a person looks typical of a country, for within any country you get so many different types, but nevertheless, these three were, as far as I was concerned, fairly typical New Zealanders. They were tall, muscular, their arms and faces reddened by wind and sun, and they looked extremely tough in their thick shirts, cord trousers and heavy boots, with their battered hats pulled down over their eyes and their rifles slung over their shoulders. They carried no gory carcasses, but this did not surprise me, for Brian had already explained that the deer corpses are left where they fall. To try to keep pests such as deer or opossums under control would mean that the Wildlife Department would have to employ a colossal band of hunters who did nothing else all day long. This, financially speaking, was impossible, but there were many people who enjoyed hunting, and from these the Department recruited their hunters, covered their out-of-pocket expenses and let them hunt in whichever areas the pests were getting out of control. This deer hunt they had just returned from (not a very good one, apparently, for they had only managed to get sixteen deer) thus fulfilled two purposes: they got the pleasure of hunting, and they were cutting down the deer population around the valley so that it did not get out of control and swamp the Takahe out of existence permanently. Presently, full of food and tea, we sat back in front of the roaring fire (for the night was bitterly cold) and I opened one of the bottles of Scotch which I had had the foresight to bring with us.

The next morning, stiff and cramped from the weird positions we had had to adopt on the floor of the hut all night, we got up and cooked breakfast. Outside, the valley was full of mist, so we could not see more than a few feet from the hut door, but Brian seemed confident that this would rise as soon as the sun got up. Breakfast over, the deer hunters left us, trudging off through the mists down the gorge towards Te Anau, where a boat was waiting for them. They had been pleasant company but we were glad to see them go, for it gave us just those few more spare inches of breathing space in the hut that we felt we could do with.

Brian's forecast was right, for by about eight o'clock the mist had lifted sufficiently for us to be able to see most of the lake and some of the surrounding mountains. It even began to look as though it was going to be a fine day and so, full of high spirits, we set off along the edge of the lake towards the great meadow of snow grass where, Brian said, the first Takahe nests had been found. As I say, we set off in high spirits, for in that milky, opalescent light the lake seemed smaller than we had imagined and our destination a mere half hour's stroll away. We were soon to learn that Takahe Valley was deceptive. In the many years that I have been hunting for animals in various parts of the world, I can never remember being so acutely uncomfortable as I was during our sojourn in Takahe Valley, and that first day was a pretty good sample of what any prospective Takahe hunter has to put up with. To begin with there were the clouds: they would drift over the edge of the mountains, take a look into the valley and decide that this was a suitable resting place, so they would pour themselves in like a slow-motion wave, enveloping both you and the landscape and drenching you to the skin. This was one of the minor irritants. The snow grass, which grew in huge, waist-high, barley-sugar coloured clumps, seemed to collect water with the enthusiasm of a sponge and then, as you pushed through the clumps, this water would be shared with you in the most generous fashion. To add to the pleasure of all this, there was the sphagnum moss. This thick, brilliant green moss grew like an extremely expensive fitted carpet around and between the snow grass clumps, looking as smooth as a bowling green and just as comfortable to walk on. True, it was thick—about six or eight inches in places—and your feet sank into it as though it were a magnificent pile carpet, but once your feet *had* sunk into it, the moss was reluctant to release its hold and it required quite an effort to extract one foot from the moss before you could take the next step. Just to make the whole thing more difficult, this mossy carpet was, of course, growing on water, so that with every step you not only got a shoe full of water, but the sound of your feet being extricated from the moss resounded with a liquid plop that echoed through the valley like a gunshot, and after half a mile of this I would not have thought there was a Takahe within fifty miles that was not appraised of our arrival and progress. So, yard by sodden yard, we progressed along the side of the lake and through the meadow of snow grass. Occasionally we would leave the snow grass and make short sorties into the edge of the beech forest, for in the non-breeding season the demarcation line where the snow grass reaches the forest seems to be a favourite haunt of the Takahe. The dark, grey-green boles of the trees

99

were covered with moisture, as were the small, dull green leaves. Here and there the branches would be festooned with great, hanging masses of lichen, like some weird coral formation along the boughs. At first sight this lichen looked white—indeed, from a distance some of the trees looked as if they were covered with snow—but on close inspection the delicate, branched filigree was a very pale greeny-grey, a delicate and rather beautiful colour.

For the rest of the day we plodded on through the damp snow grass and through the gloomy beech woods with their Martian growths of lichen. We were icy cold and drenched to the skin, and we found just about everything except a Takahe. We found fresh droppings at one stage and clustered round them with all the mixed feelings that Robinson Crusoe had when he discovered the famous footprint; we found places where the birds had recently been feeding, shredding the long stalks of snow grass through the beaks; we even found empty nests, placed on the ground and constructed out of snow grass, each one cunningly concealed under the drooping stalks of a massive clump of grass; Brian, at one point, even said that he *heard* a Takahe, but as it was growing towards evening and the valley was so silent you could hear a pin drop, we thought he was merely saying this to cheer us up. At length the weather started to close down on us and the light became too bad for photography, even supposing there had been anything to photograph. We were right down the far end of the valley by now and Brian thought we ought to turn back for, as he pointed out cheerfully, if a cloud descended into the valley suddenly we might well get lost and have to spend the night wandering round in ever decreasing circles, up to our waists in wet snow grass. Spurred on by this horrid thought, we retraced, with considerable distaste, our squishy footprints through the meadow and along the shores of

he lake. When we reached the hut about which we had been
o disparaging the day before, we were so tired, cold, wet and
lispirited that it seemed the very height of luxury. To be
ıble to strip off our wet clothes and sit in front of a roaring
og fire, gulping hot tea liberally laced with whisky, was
:cstasy, and we were very soon telling ourselves that today
ıad been an exception. The bad weather conditions had
made the Takahe more than normally secretive. The follow-
ng day, we assured each other, the valley would be so full of
Takahe that we would hardly be able to walk.

Our enthusiastic mood was somewhat marred, but not
ıltogether shattered, when Jim's wet socks (carefully hung on
our improvised line over the fire to dry) fell with deadly
ıccuracy into the saucepan of soup that Brian was meditatively
tirring. However, the soup seemed none the worse for the
ıddition of this slightly macabre ingredient, and it gave Jim
one more thing to complain about, which he did with the
ıtmost vigour.

The following morning the weather looked, if anything,
lightly worse than it had the previous day; however, we
:limbed, shivering, into our still-moist clothes and set off along
he shores of the lake once again. Once more we reached the
meadow and plunged into the icy grasp of the snow grass
ınd sphagnum moss, and once more we found signs of Takahe
out did not get a glimpse of a bird. By the time mid-afternoon
:ame the weather was getting increasingly bad, and we were
n a mood of the blackest depression. We knew we should
ıave to leave the valley the following day and it seemed heart-
breaking to have come so far and to have got so wet and cold
or nothing. It was not as if the birds were not there: the
tripped snow grass we found was fresh, as were the droppings.
The wretched birds were obviously playing hide-and-seek
with us, but in that type of country and in our sort of mood,

we were not feeling like playing games. Then, just after
had slipped and fallen heavily into a particularly glutinou
patch of wet sphagnum moss, Brian suddenly held up hi
hand for silence. We stood there, hardly daring to breathe
while our feet sank slowly and steadily into the moss.

'What is it?' I whispered at last.

'Takahe,' said Brian.

'Are you sure?' I asked, for I had heard nothing except the
splash and squelch of my own fall.

'Yes,' said Brian. 'Listen and you'll hear them.'

We had been working our way along the edge of the valley,
some twenty yards from where the beech forest started its
precipitous climb up the mountainside, and here the clumps
of snow grass seemed larger and grew more closely together
than in other areas we had searched. We stood in a silent,
frozen, dripping group and listened. Suddenly, to our right
among the beech trees, we heard the noise that Brian had
heard. It was a deep, throbbing, drum-like noise, very similar
to the noise that the Wekas had made on Kapiti but magnified a hundredfold and with a rich, almost contralto quality
about it. There were some seven or eight rapid drum-beats,
a brief silence, and then another series from a bit further away.
Something moved in the snow grass ahead of us and then
something else moved, nearer the beech forest. Oblivious
of the struggles that Chris and Jim were having with camera
and tripod, I drifted with Brian towards these movements.
I say drifted because this is what we tried to do, but to my
over-sensitive ears our feet were making as much noise in the
sphagnum moss as an exceptionally large troupe of hippo-
potami suffering from in-growing toenails walking through a
huge cauldron of extremely thick porridge. Gradually we got
closer and closer to the spot where we had seen the movement,
then the snow grass quivered again and we froze. After a

moment we moved forward cautiously, for the quiver had only been some twenty feet away from us. Again the grass moved, and I shifted my position slightly. Then, quite suddenly, from behind a large clump of snow grass, a Takahe appeared.

I was completely taken aback for, only having seen black-and white photographs of the Takahe, I was imagining something about the size of an English Moorhen, with the sombre, mottled plumage of the Weka, but there stood a bird the size of a large turkey—but more rotund in shape—and against the background of dark beech leaves and pale blonde snow grass, he glowed like a jewel. He had a heavy, almost finch-like beak that, like his legs, was scarlet; his head and breast were a rich, Mediterranean blue, and his back and wings a misty dragon green. He stood straddle-legged among the snow grass, cocked his head at me and made his drumming noise. I gazed at him with admiration, and he looked back at me with the deepest suspicion. Presently, having examined me carefully, he bobbed his head and then slowly, and with immense dignity, he stepped carefully round a clump of snow grass and disappeared. What I should have done, of course, was to remain still and he would probably have appeared again, but so anxious was I not to lose sight of this magnificent bird that I took a few steps to the side to try and keep him in view. This was my undoing. He gave a startled glance over his shoulder, uttered a deep grunt of alarm and started to run swiftly but slightly flat-footedly towards the shelter of the beech trees. He disappeared into the gloom of the trees and then all we could hear were surreptitious crackling and agitated drummings, but no amount of careful stalking on our part enabled us to catch another glimpse of the birds.

By now the weather had closed down on us to such an extent that Brian insisted we made for the hut, so, cold and wet but happy that we had at last achieved success—however slight—we wended our way through the snow grass and along the lake's edge. We had nearly reached the end of the lake, and the warmth of the hut was within half a mile of us (we could see the curl of welcoming smoke from the tall stack) when Brian turned and looked over his shoulder.

'Look at that,' he said, 'that's the sort of thing I didn't want us to get caught in.'

At the very far end of the valley, just appearing over the rim of tree-covered mountains, was a great, grey fist of cloud. As we stood and watched, it curved over the mountain tops and then poured down the sides into the valley with a speed that had to be seen to be believed. Within seconds the area in which we had seen the Takahe had disappeared completely; within a few more seconds the snow grass meadows at the other end of the lake had vanished under the muffling grey paw; then the cloud flattened out over the smooth lake surface and came racing towards us, swallowing up the valley as it came. We got to the door of the hut as the first wisps started to coil and twist round us, and as we opened the door thankfully and looked back, Takahe Valley had been obliterated as if it had never been there, and we were looking at a blank wall of swirling grey cloud. Taking it all round we agreed that we were extremely lucky not to have been caught at the other end of the lake and so, while the cloud pressed coldly against the window of the hut, we piled the fire high with dry wood, stripped off our wet things and lay about in the pink glow of the flames, sipping whisky and tea in equal proportions, all feeling vastly satisfied in an obscure way that we had seen the Takahe and cheated the elements.

'Well,' said Brian at length, 'tomorrow we'll walk down to Te Anau and then we can go up to Mount Bruce. You'll get some good shots of the Takahe up there. Once they outgrew the bantam they became terribly tame, they're almost domestic now.'

'What I can't understand,' said Jim, 'is why we didn't go to Mount Bruce in the first place, instead of mucking about up here, risking pneumonia.'

'It wouldn't have been authentic,' said Chris austerely. 'We wanted to show the bird's real environment . . . get the feel of the place.'

'Well, I certainly got the feel of the place,' said Jim, thoughtfully squeezing about half a cupful of water out of one of his socks.

The next morning the cloud had lifted and the whole valley was as clear as crystal, bathed in morning sunshine. We collected our gear together and set off early, for it was a long climb down the mountainside to Te Anau, where the boat was to meet us. As we made our way down through the dripping beech forest, slipping and sliding on the thick carpet of dead, wet beech leaves, I marvelled at the patience and skill of the little group of men who had climbed up this almost sheer mountainside, carrying on their backs a bantam to save the Takahe with. I only wished, as I sat down heavily for the third time and slid several hundred feet on my backside, that there were more people in the world who would devote this sort of time and energy to the saving of a species.

Now that we had actually seen the Takahe in its own valley I was anxious that Brian should take us to Mount Bruce where the Takahe chicks, so laboriously obtained from the valley, now lived. The sanctuary is, of course, Government-run, and it consists of a large and nicely overgrown area—carefully fenced—and planted with snow grass. Here the Takahes, now fully adult birds, lived in complete freedom. When we went into the fenced area there was no sign of Takahe, but as soon as they heard our voices they appeared out of the undergrowth and ran towards us, heads down, their great feet thumping the ground. They gathered around us, barging and pushing and almost climbing into our laps in their eagerness to take the banana we had brought for them. Seen at close range like this their colouring was even more brilliant than I had imagined, and the greeny-gold and purple of their silken feathering gleamed in the sun with a dazzling opalescence. It was a great privilege, having live Takahe feeding from your hand and clustering around your feet like domestic fowl, but an even greater privilege was in store.

In one corner of the Takahe paddock was a large aviary, shaped not unlike a half-moon. We had been so busy concentrating on the Takahe that I had given this structure scant attention, beyond peering into it casually. As all I could see in it were some twigs and numerous clumps of grass, I had presumed it was deserted. Now, disentangling myself with difficulty from the Takahes, who were convinced that I still had some bananas concealed about my person, I asked Brian whether the aviary had, in fact, been built for the Takahe when they were younger.

'No,' said Brian with considerable pride, 'that is a Kakaporium.'

'What,' I enquired cautiously, 'is a Kakaporium?'

'It is a place,' explained Brian, watching my face closely, 'where one keeps Kakapos.'

The effect it had on me was much the same as if he had casually announced that he had a stable full of multi-coloured unicorns, for the Kakapo is not only one of the rarest of the New Zealand birds, but one of the most unusual, and though I had longed to see one I had thought it would be an impossibility.

'Do you mean to say,' I asked, 'that you have in that aviary a Kakapo and that you never even *mentioned* it to me?'

'That's right,' said Brian, grinning. 'Surprise.'

'Lead me to it,' I demanded, quivering with eagerness, 'lead me to it this instant.'

Amused and pleased by my wild excitement, Brian opened the door of the aviary and we went inside. Over in one corner there was a wooden box over which had been stacked a large pile of dried heather. We approached this and cautiously parted the heather, and I was staring, from a range of about eighteen inches, into the face of a real, live Kakapo.

The Kakapo's other name is Owl Parrot, and this is singularly apt, for even a professional ornithologist could be pardoned for mistaking it for an owl at first glance. It is large—bigger than a Barn Owl—and its plumage is a lovely, misty, sage green, flecked with black. It has a large, flattened

facial mask like an owls, from which peer two enormous dark eyes. This particular specimen glared at me with all the malignancy of an elderly colonel who had been woken up in his club by a drunken subaltern. Apart from its appearance, which is strange enough, the Kakapo has two other attributes that make it unusual. First, although it can fly rather clumsily, it rarely does, spending most of its time running about the ground in the most un-parrot-like fashion, and second, as if this was not enough, it is nocturnal. In the wild state they wear little tracks through the grass with their nightly perambulations, so that the undergrowth in a Kakapo area looks like innumerable, interlacing country lanes seen from the air. As we filmed the glaring Kakapo, Brian told me that its status in the wild state was precarious in the extreme—so precarious, in fact, that this bird might be the very last Kakapo left alive. To anyone—even someone not particularly interested in birds—this was a sobering and unpleasant thought, particularly as one knew that the Kakapo was not alone among the birds, mammals and the reptiles of this world in being in this frightful predicament. Probably the only hope of survival the Kakapo and the Takahe have is in sanctuaries like Mount Bruce, and the more countries that start this kind of establishment, the better it will be.

Now that we had filmed the Takahe story we intended to spend our last three days in New Zealand in and around Wellington, filming anything of interest that we found. However, at this point, Fate, in the shape of a small man in a bar, stepped in and disorganised all our plans.

Ever since we had been in New Zealand two things had haunted and depressed Chris beyond measure. The first was that it seemed impossible for him to get a decent recording of anything, for the moment he got the recorder out and set up, either the subject would fly away or else a car would pass or a 'plane would fly overhead or a stiff breeze would spring up, or one of the hundred and one things would happen that make recording impossible. The second thing was that everywhere we went in New Zealand people asked us what we had filmed, and when we told them they all said in astonishment, 'But haven't you filmed the Keas?... You can't do a programme on New Zealand without the Keas . . . the Clowns of the Snowline, they call them . . . and they'd be so *easy* to film . . . they're naturally tame and you find them simply everywhere.'

Well, other people might have found these large and spectacular parrots everywhere, but up to that point we had not seen a single specimen, and this had irritated Chris beyond measure. So when this small, unfortunate man in the bar asked us what we had filmed so far, a Llama-like look came over Chris's face as I recited the list.

'What?' asked the little man in astonishment. 'Haven't you filmed any Keas?'

'No!' said Chris, compressing into that one humble word enough coldness to start a small iceberg.

'Well, you should go up to Mount Cook,' said the little man, not realising how closely he was tiptoeing towards death. 'I've just come from there—plenty of 'em there. Can't leave anything about, they'll be straight down and tear it to pieces. Regular comedians they are . . . you should really try and film those, you know.'

I hastily filled Chris's glass.

'Yes, well, we are going to try,' I said.

'Yes,' said Chris suddenly, loudly and defiantly, 'and we're leaving for Mount Cook tomorrow.'

He drained his glass with a flourish and glared at our thunderstruck faces.

'But we can't,' said Brian. 'We haven't got enough time left.'

'I refuse to leave New Zealand until I have filmed Keas,' barked Chris, and so, faced with such an ultimatum, what could we do? We went to Mount Cook. Here we stayed in another lavish Government hotel with a magnificent view out over Mount Cook and the Tasman glacier, and started on a frantic, last-minute search for Keas. Everyone assured us it would be very easy; the mountains around, they said, were full of Keas, every valley bulged with them. You could not park your car for fear that several dozen would descend on it and take it to pieces with the enthusiasm of mad motor mechanics. All you had to do was to go anywhere up into the surrounding mountains—but simply *anywhere*—and shout 'Kea . . . kea . . . kea . . .' in imitation of their cries, and before you knew where you were, Keas were swooping down on you from all directions. Well, we tried. The day of our arrival we drove round and round Mount Cook, stopping at every conceivable crevasse and crag to shout 'Kea . . . kea . . . kea . . .' in the prescribed manner, but the barren terrain remained Kea-less. That night, in spite of excellent wine and a delicately grilled trout, Chris persisted in looking like a disgruntled camel that had forgotten the directions to the nearest waterhole.

The following morning, at a most indecent hour and in depressed silence, we drove up to the foot of Mount Cook, where the Tasman glacier lies, to resume our futile Kea hunt. The road up to this weird area, which looks like a small section of the moon, resembles a dried-up river bed, and it eventually peters out on a cliff edge with below the great glacier and above the snow-capped peak of Mount Cook. At this point the glacier was wide—a great sheet of thick, carunculated ice filled, like a fruit cake, with the débris it collected in its passage: rocks, stones, tree trunks and, doubtless, the frozen corpses of innumerable Keas. Standing above it we could *hear* the glacier moving, squeaking, groaning and scrunching to itself as it crept forward, millimetre by millimetre, down the valley to its rendezvous with the sea.

Raising our voices above the conversation of the glacier we shouted 'Kea' at the barren, deserted landscape and listened to it being echoed back derisively from every hand. Then, to our complete astonishment, a genuine Kea suddenly

appeared out of nowhere and perched on a rocky pinnacle
well out of camera range. Chris, his eyes bulging with
emotion, stumbled up the slope towards the bird, uttering
hoarse Kea cries. The Kea took one look at this dishevelled,
wild-eyed figure staggering out of the glacier, uttered what
can only be described as a disbelieving scream of horror and
promptly flew away. When we had recovered from our
unseemly laughter we discovered, to our amazement, that,
far from discouraging Chris, he was now full of enthusiasm
at having caught this glimpse of the Kea in its natural habitat.
He felt that success was within our grasp, and so all we had
to do now was film the approach shots. By this he meant
the shots of the Land-Rover arriving at the glacier, us getting
out and shouting for Keas, and various shots of the terrain.
Then, when we had our close-up shots of the Keas, the two
would fit together. Filming is a curious, upside-down sort of
business and frequently one has to film a departure before you
film the arrival. So all the camera gear was unshipped and
erected and then, as it was to be a sound shot, Chris solemnly
got the recorder out and mounted it on a pile of stones.

After much running to and fro with cables and micro-
phones, he proclaimed that he was ready. Our job was
simple: we had to drive the Land-Rover to a given point, get
out and start to shout for Keas, our action being picked up
by the camera whilst the recorder captured for posterity the
sounds of our voices echoing back from the mountains.
Now, as I have said, you could not wish for a more desolate
and deserted spot. Not only was there no human being or
human habitation in sight, but there was no animal life either,
so it was with considerable astonishment—when we left the
Land-Rover and started to call for the Keas—to hear a sudden
clanking uproar that sounded like a Ford factory gone mad.
It was the scream and grind and crash of machinery tortured

beyond belief. None of us could imagine what was causing the noise or where it was coming from. All we knew was that Chris was squatting by the recorder, earphones clapped to his ears, with a look of disbelieving anguish on his face.

Then, from around a great tumbled heap of rocks, there appeared an enormous vehicle, the great-grandfather of all bulldozers, a gigantic thing half the size of a house which shuddered and roared and clanked its way towards us, while perched on a tiny saddle on top was a small, grizzled man who appeared to have some slight control over it. He waved to us cheerily as the monstrous machine shuddered towards us. Chris tore off the earphones and rushed up to the side of the juggernaut, waving his arms wildly.

'Shut it off,' he screamed, 'we're trying to record a sound take.'

'Aye?' yelled the little man, changing gear with a screech that made the blood run cold.

'We're filming . . . can't you shut it off?' bellowed Chris, now purple in the face.

'You'll have to speak louder . . . can't hear,' explained the little man.

'Turn the bloody thing off . . . TURN IT OFF!' screamed Chris, making wild gestures. The little man gazed at him thoughtfully, played another brief but excrutiating tune on his gear box, and then leant forward and pressed a switch and the great machine fell silent.

'Now, what were you saying?' he enquired. 'Sorry I couldn't hear you very well up here—it's a bit noisy.'

Chris drew a deep, shuddering breath.

'Could you keep that . . . that . . . thing switched off for a few minutes? You see, we're making a film and trying to record sound.'

'Oh, a film, eh?' said the little man interestedly. 'Yes, sure I can keep her off.'

'Thank you,' said Chris shakily, and went back to the recorder. He had just put the earphones back on and given us the signal to begin when the monstrous machine suddenly started up again, only now, by some magical means, the little man had put it into reverse and it was slowly disappearing behind the pile of rocks from whence it had sprung. Chris, his face now congested to the colour of an over-ripe peach, flung the earphones on the ground and, mouthing what appeared to be terse phrases of a sort which no BBC producer is supposed to know, pursued the gigantic machine behind the rock pile. After a moment, blessed silence reigned and Chris reappeared from behind the rocks, mopping his brow.

'Now,' he said in a hoarse voice, 'we'll try it once more.'

This time we did succeed in getting the shot, but the episode had its detrimental effect on Chris's nerves and he tended to leap like a startled deer at the slightest noise for the rest of the day. His condition was not improved by the fact that we did not see any more Keas and so we returned to the hotel seeped in the deepest gloom. In fact, so depressed did we look that our charming Maori maid was moved to enquire tenderly what was the matter. Delighted at having a sympathetic audience, we all spoke at once. When the babble had subsided somewhat and she could make out what we were talking about, she looked at us in amazement.

'Keas?' she said bewildered. 'You've been trying to film Keas? But why didn't you tell me?'

'Why?' asked Chris, suspiciously.

'I've got five wild ones that come down to the back of the hotel every morning,' she said. 'I feed them on bread and butter. Every morning they're there.'

As an anti-climax this left little to be desired.

The next morning at dawn we prowled around the back of the hotel armed with cameras, tape recorders and a lavish supply of bread and butter which, in some mysterious way, managed to adhere itself to almost every piece of equipment and most of our clothing; sure enough, when the morning mists rose and Mount Cook appeared, its snowcap pink in the morning sun, we heard the wild cries echoing among the rocks at the foot of the ridge of mountains that rose at the back of the hotel. They were, in essence, not unlike the cries that we, at the risk of acute laryngitis, had attempted to emulate, but they had a wild, ringing, exuberant quality about them that we could never have matched. Very soon the five Keas appeared, flew on to the roof of the hotel, and proceeded to march up and down, watching us and shouting 'Kea . . . kea . . . arrrar' at intervals. Their strutting, pompous walk, their general attitude of being the lords of all they surveyed, combined with this oft-repeated and never varying cry, made them remind me irresistibly of a small group of Fascists. At first sight they looked very like the Kakas we had seen on Kapiti, but as the sun rose I could see that, although they were like them in shape, they were quite different in coloration. Basically, the Kea's plumage is a melody of greens, ranging from grass green to sage, but with a purplish bloom to it that, from a distance, makes them look quite dark. The underside of the wing is the most beautiful, clear flame orange, and when the bird spreads its wings, or takes flight, it looks as though it has, for one brief moment, burst into flames.

Having at long last arrived within camera range, the Keas proceeded to give us a wonderful performance. They engulfed bread and butter in vast quantities, they ran along the guttering of the hotel and hung upside down, shouting, and then took it in turns to skid down the slope of the roof like children on a snow slide. They yelled and screamed and engulfed more bread and butter, and then tried valiantly but unsuccessfully to remove the top from the Land-Rover. Tiring of this engineering feat, two of them flew off and went and shouted 'Kea!' loudly and shrilly outside every bedroom window they could find, while the rest of them dismantled a fascinating pile of cardboard boxes they discovered outside the back door of the hotel. They were irresponsible, noisy, devilish and altogether charming birds, and as I watched two of them, their beaks covered with bread and butter, fighting over the privilege of sliding down a roof, screaming abuse at each other, crests up and wings flapping so that the orange feathering glowed in the sun, making them look more like an animated bonfire than anything, I reflected what a pity it was that, charming though I found him, the Kea was considered by many in New Zealand to be Public Enemy Number One. Keas have developed a taste for the fat of that domestic animal which comes closer to a New Zealander's heart than his mother: the sheep.

Now, when he finds the skin of a sheep, or even the corpse of one, there is no doubt that the Kea will feast on the fat, but the sheep farmers insist that he does more than this—that he actually attacks and kills living sheep to get at the fat. There *are* authentic cases of Keas having done this, but whether all Keas do it, and whether—if they do—they produce the amount of damage that the farmers claim, is a subject that has never been scientifically investigated. Tell the average sheep farmer this, or elaborate it by saying that you think it's worth losing a few sheep for the pleasure of having the Keas around, and you are qualifying yourself for a swift ambulance ride. And yet the Kea—large, beautiful, noisy, full of character and mischievousness—personifies the wild mountain country of

New Zealand. He is a gay and wicked clown, a bird to be proud of. Instead of which there is—as there is for so many nice things in this life—a price on his head, and he is shot wherever he is found.

As a last vignette of New Zealand I offer you this: a backdrop of Mount Cook, wearing a tattered hat of pink snow; wisps of morning mist drifting languidly along the mountainsides, coiling gently round the great boulders, covering the scars made by recent landslides; and flying against it, arrow swift and eager, a group of Keas, their wings flashing in the sun, their joyful shouts of 'Kea . . . kea . . . *kea*' echoing and ringing among the ancient rocks.

THE
ATTIC OF THE WORLD

Distinguishing those that have feathers, and bite
From those that have whiskers, and scratch.
Hunting of the Snark

THE ARRIVAL

THE GOOD SHIP *Wanganella* that carried us staunchly from
New Zealand was, without doubt, one of the most charming
vessels I have ever travelled in. I decided at length that it
must have been designed by an economy-minded film company who had wanted to try to get as many styles as possible,
ranging from Elizabethan to slick nineteen-twenty décor
(taking in the worst of the French kings and the Edwardians
en route), into one ship. Everywhere you went there were
doors labelled 'Tudor Lounge' or 'The Palm Snuggery', and,
to your astonishment, when you opened the door there really
was a Tudor Lounge or a Palm Snuggery. It was worth
travelling on the ship just to see the mosaic pillars in the
dining saloon, which were of such ostentatious vulgarity
that they were charming. It was on this interior decorator's
nightmare of a vessel that we met Gert.

When we had completed dinner and finished admiring the
mosaic columns, we went into a sort of Shakespearean library,
full of oak beams and faded bound copies of *Punch*, to have
our coffee. As we drank we surveyed such of our fellow
passengers as were visible, with a practised eye, for after a
few years' travelling on ships you develop a sort of sixth sense
about which passenger is going to turn out to be the ship's
bore and which one is going to try to inveigle you into deck
games and so forth. After a slow and careful scrutiny, I
turned to Jacquie.

'There is only one person here worth cultivating,' I said firmly.

'Which one?' asked Chris, who was new to this game.

'The one sitting over there under the Tudor warming-pan.'

Chris and Jacquie surveyed my choice and then turned to me in astonishment. They were not altogether to be blamed, for at first glance the woman I had selected looked not unlike a medium-sized hippopotamus clad entirely in pink and wearing a blonde wig of a hue that would have put any over-ripe cornfield to shame. Her small, fat hands, glittering with rings, clasped a glass full of what appeared to be gin, and she stared into space out of circular blue eyes so heavily ringed with mascara that she had the appearance of a doll.

'You're nuts!' said Chris, with conviction.

'He just can't resist blondes of any size,' explained Jacquie.

'I'll prove to you I'm right,' I said and walked over to where my choice sat, still staring moodily at the oak beams.

'Good evening,' I said, 'sorry to worry you, but can you give me a light?'

'What the bloody hell for?' she enquired with interest. 'I saw you light your bleeding fag with a lighter five minutes ago.' Her voice was rich and foggy, the sort of voice that only comes by years of tender application of gin to the vocal cords. I decided that I had underestimated the alertness of my lady friend.

'I just thought you looked nice,' I confessed, 'and I wanted to have a drink with you.'

'Cor, picking me up at my age—you've got a bleeding sauce,' she said with amusement.

'Oh, it's quite all right,' I said hastily, 'that's my wife over there.'

She shifted her ample bottom slightly so that she could

crane round a particularly repulsive aspidistra and see our table.

'All right,' she said, giving me a sudden mischievous and strangely sweet smile, 'I'll 'ave a drink with you . . . at least you all look alive . . . dead crowd of bleeders I've seen so far on this ship.'

She surged to her feet and waddled across the room in front of me, and then, introductions having been made, she wedged herself into a chair with certain difficulty, and beamed at us all impartially. When drinks had arrived, she seized her glass and held it aloft.

"Ere's 'ow,' she said, drank deeply, stifled a small and lady-like belch, patted her mouth with a scrap of lace handkerchief and settled herself so deeply and tightly in her chair that I felt nothing short of explosive would ever remove her from it.

'It's nice to be matey,' she said, just loudly enough to be clearly heard by the people at the next table. 'There was I thinking what a toffee-nosed lot of bastards there was on board, and then along you comes.'

That moment set the seal on our trip aboard the *Wanganella*, for Gert turned out to be all that I had anticipated and more. Thrice married and now a widow, she had been, during her years in Australia, practically everything one could think of, but the two most unlikely and likely callings were those of doctor's receptionist and barmaid. In the latter capacity she had met with the success she obviously deserved, and now owned her own pub in some remote part of Australia. But it was Gert's medical abilities that fascinated us more than anything. During her time with the unfortunate doctor who employed her she must have driven him very close to a nervous breakdown, for she had been utterly convinced that his ability to diagnose was non-existent, and that any treatment he saw fit to recommend to his customers was based on this faulty diagnosis plus an insufficient knowledge of how the human frame functioned. She had, however, picked up a wonderful series of medical malapropisms, the origins of which she must have learnt from her wretched employer.

"E 'ad no confidence, that was 'is trouble,' she confessed to us. "E was a bloody nice bloke, but 'e 'ad no confidence. I always said to 'im, I said, "you 'ave no confidence, cock, you're always passing the bleeding buck to others." Now, a woman would come to 'im with a bun in the oven. Perfectly ordinary, *you'd* say, but no, off 'e'd pack 'er to a geologist.'

'A what?' we would enquire, breathless with anticipation.

'A geologist . . . you know . . . one of them fancy bleeders that thinks they know all about females' guts . . . prod about your ovaloids and there's five guineas up the shoot.'

Gert on almost any medical subject was gorgeous.

"Ad a Yid come once, said 'e wanted 'is bleeding flap off. I said I thought they did that at birth with Yids, but 'e said no, that 'is family had defecated and become Christins and now 'e wanted to become a bleeding Yid again. So, anyway, we took 'is flap off and I went to see 'im in hospital . . . thought 'e'd feel a bit strange, see? Cor, the bleeding fuss . . . you'd think we'd taken the bleeding lot off. I told 'im 'e was lucky not to catch that elephantus . . . saw a picture of that in one of the Doc's books once . . . bloke with a screw-tum the size of this chair . . . 'ad to carry it around in a sort of cart thing . . . blimey, I says to this Yid, think yourself lucky. Trouble with 'alf these people, they don't know 'ow lucky they are.'

I wondered how many of them realised how lucky they were to have Gert around when they were ill.

So, aided by Gert and the exquisite décor of the ship, we passed a very pleasant Alice-in-Wonderland type voyage, until the *Wanganella* finally, and with a great flourish, landed us at Sydney. As we were landing we were treated to one final burst from Gert. A female of indeterminate age had been, throughout the voyage, flaunting her one and only asset at any and every man she could find, and this Gert had watched with the sternest disapproval. It so happened that this female, carrying, as it were, all before her, was going down the gangway ahead of us. Gert, thrusting her pink moon face over the rail for a final goodbye, caught sight of the well-endowed (whether by nature or artifice) female ahead of us. Her face pursed up into a look of disapproval as she followed the female's bulging descent of the gangway. Then she looked at us and winked.

'Finest set of mummery glands now arriving in Australia,' she bellowed happily.

The success of our arrival was assured after that.

CHAPTER 4

Lyrebirds and Leadbeaters

They sought it with thimbles, they sought it with care;
They pursued it with forks and hope.

Hunting of the Snark

WE ALL FELL IN LOVE WITH AUSTRALIA completely and instantly. If ever I was compelled to settle down in one spot —which God forbid—Australia is one of the few countries I have visited that I could choose.

We drove down from Sydney to Melbourne under a brilliant blue sky striped with fragile wisps of cloud. The countryside was rolling, sun-bleached grassland, with here and there the rust-red earth showing through. Dotted about were copses of eucalyptus trees, their trunks—from the distance—gleaming white in the sun like bleached bones. They are extraordinarily beautiful and graceful trees that manage to contort their trunks and limbs into the most incredible postures, so that they look as though they are taking part in some fantastic ballet. On some of the older trees the bark was peeling off, hanging down in great, beard-like festoons, the new bark underneath having a delicate pink glow when you examined it closely, so that you could almost imagine that the trunk was modelled out of flesh. Towards evening on the second day we stopped to have some tea. In the great, golden grassfield there was a group of dead eucalyptus standing, their trunks and branches as brilliant white as coral, and meandering through them the rough red road up which we had driven the Land-Rover. The sinking sun was washing the whole scene in a delicate yellowish haze and suddenly, out of nowhere, a flock of six Galah Cockatoos appeared, swooping down out of the sky to land in the dead trees above us. Seen in that light and against the background of the brilliant white tree trunks, they were incredibly beautiful, with their white crests, pale ash-grey wings and rich, dusty pink bodies and faces. They ambled along the branches in the faintly reptilian way that members of the parrot family have, peering down at us, muttering incoherently and raising their crests. As we did not move but sat spellbound, watching them, they eventually decided that we were harmless and they flew down on to the ground in a tumble of pink and grey feathers that made them look like bundles of rose petals. They settled on the red earth and slowly waddled along to where, in a deep tyre track, a pool of rainwater gleamed, and there they drank greedily. Then one of them found a delectable morsel in a grass tuft and a disgraceful fight broke out over its ownership. They yarred at each other with open beaks, circling round and flapping their ash-grey wings. Eventually they flew off in a swift, arrow-like flight, their breasts gleaming against the blue sky. Galahs are one of the smaller, but one of the most beautiful of Australia's cockatoos, and as I watched them wheeling against the sky I wondered how anyone could have the heart to shoot them, and yet I knew that in certain areas they are considered a pest and are shot in vast quantities every year.

As we drew closer to Melbourne the weather grew colder and colder until, by the time we had arrived in the city, it was as cold as Manchester on a raw November day. I was—quite stupidly—unprepared for this kind of weather in

Australia. I had imagined it to be a land of perpetual sunshine, although a glance at an atlas and a few calculations would have shown me how wrong I was. Luckily we had brought plenty of clothing to cope with the inclement weather in New Zealand, and this now stood us in good stead.

The two things that we were most anxious to see and to film, if possible, were the Lyrebirds and the Leadbeater's Possum. The Lyrebird is probably one of the most spectacular of the Australian birds, and I knew that the Wildlife Department of Melbourne had created a sanctuary for them at a place called Sherbrooke Forest, but even when you have created a sanctuary for some animal it does not mean that the creature is necessarily going to be easy to see or film. However, Mr. Butcher, the head of the Wildlife Department, seemed to think that we had a good chance of success, and passed us over to the capable guidance of Miss Ira Watson, who had been doing studies on the birds and knew the area intimately. Ira had booked rooms for us at a small hotel situated on the edge of the sanctuary, so early one crisp, cold morning, we set off with our mountains of equipment. By the time we had settled in the hotel, however, and unpacked our gear the whole world had been enveloped in grey mist and drizzle, and the temperature appeared to have dropped well below zero. Reluctant and shivering, we picked up our equipment and followed Ira into the forest in search of Lyrebirds.

The forest consisted of giant, elderly eucalyptus trees, standing about in elegant attitudes, each one festooned with its shawl of tattered and peeling bark. Interspersed among these were giant tree ferns, squatting on hairy brown trunks, their long fronds bursting from the top like a feathery green fountain. The whole forest was gloomy, mist shrouded and as echoing as a deserted cathedral. Ira took us along a narrow, meandering path which presently led us out into a sort of wide ride through the forest. The floor of the ride was covered with tree ferns and short vegetation, and here, in a clearing, we piled all the equipment into a heap and then set off to look for Lyrebirds.

The Lyrebird is not particularly spectacular to look at, resembling a rather drab hen pheasant. Its beauty lies in its tail, which consists of two long, delicately curved white feathers which curve out and round so that they resemble an ancient lyre. To add verisimilitude to the illusion, the area between these two immense, lyre-shaped feathers is criss-crossed with a delicate tracery of fine white feathers that resemble the strings of the lyre. At the beginning of the breeding season the cock birds choose areas in the forest which they convert into dance halls. The area is cleared with the aid of the bird's strong feet, and the leafmould neatly piled up in the centre of the clearing as a sort of stage. When this is ready the cock bird can commence his display, and it is probably one of the most spectacular in the world. With the aid of his tail and his voice he endeavours to seduce every female Lyrebird within hearing, and even if they could resist his tail, it is doubtful that they could remain unmoved by his song. He is the most accomplished mimic and incorporates into his repertoire the songs of other birds and, indeed, any other sounds he hears which take his fancy; the result is not the cacophony you might expect but a breathtakingly beautiful performance.

We wandered through the damp undergrowth for some time and saw plenty of signs of Lyrebirds in the shape of scratchings in the leafmould and droppings, and this encouraged us. Presently we came upon one of the dancing halls and I was surprised at its size, for it measured some eight feet in diameter and the mound in the middle was about two foot six high.

'This is one of Old Spotty's halls,' said Ira. 'He's one of the oldest and tamest of the birds here. He's the one I was hoping we would find because he'd be much easier to film than the others.'

But there was no sign of Old Spotty, or of any other Lyrebirds, as we continued our way through the tree ferns. Soon we came to a small valley where the tree ferns grew thickly among massive boulders, each one wearing a green fur coat of moss. Here a tiny stream tinkled and bubbled among the boulders and occasionally, where it curved, there would be a tiny beach of white sand. It was as we were investigating this stream that we saw our first Lyrebird. Ira, who was leading, stopped suddenly and held up her hand. Very cautiously we moved up behind her and she pointed at a tiny beach by the stream some fifty feet away. On it stood a Lyrebird, his head slightly to one side as he regarded us with large, liquid dark eyes, his huge tail flowing out behind him like a waterfall of crisply starched lace. He watched us for some time and then, deciding that we must be harmless, stalked gracefully off the small beach and made his way through the tree ferns' massive trunks, pausing every now and then to scratch at the leafmould vigorously with his large feet. We followed him for some time, hoping that he might change direction and wend his way into the ride, for down there in the valley it was too dark for photography, but he was intent on his feeding and merely moved deeper and deeper into the gloom of the trees. But the fact that we had actually seen a Lyrebird cheered us up immensely, and we made our way back to the ride in much better spirits. After some hot coffee to thaw us out, we split up and started to quarter the edge of the forest along the ride.

We were so keyed up to look for Lyrebirds that it came as a considerable surprise to meet up with other inhabitants of the

forest. The first of these were three fat young Kookaburras, or Laughing Jackasses as these giant kingfishers are called in Australia. The three of them were sitting side by side on a branch, squatting there smugly in their chocolate and grey plumage, with their handsome blue wing patches gleaming. The dark mask of feathering across the eyes made them look absurdly like a trio of fat small boys who were playing bandits. To our astonishment, as soon as they saw us they uttered their wild, chattering cries and flew straight down on to the path, settling a few feet away from us. Here they hopped about, uttering wheezy cries, fluttering their wings and opening their big broad beaks in supplication. Ira, who was obviously more used to the idiosyncrasies of Sherbrooke Forest than we were, unperturbedly produced from her pocket a large piece of cheese, and with this unlikely substance we proceeded to feed the squawking babies. At last, bloated with cheese (and having made sure that we had no more on us), they flew heavily back to their ambush and sat there to await fresh victims.

The next inhabitant of the forest was even more unexpected than the Kookaburras had been. I was standing at the edge of the undergrowth, moodily wondering which way was the best to go in search of Lyrebirds, when there was a faint crackling of twigs and a portly grey animal about the size of a large bulldog suddenly shuffled out of the undergrowth. I recognised it instantly as a Wombat, for in the past (when I had been a keeper at Whipsnade Zoo) I had once had a long and passionate love affair with one of these enchanting animals, and I have been enamoured of the species ever since. Superficially they resemble Koala Bears, but are, in fact, much more stocky and bear-like in appearance, since they are adapted to ground living. They have short, strong legs—slightly bowed —which give them a rolling gait very reminiscent of a bear; but their heads look more like a Koala, with round boot-button eyes, oval plush-like nose patches, and a tattered fringe round the edge of the ears. The Wombat, having appeared out of the undergrowth, paused for a moment and then sneezed violently and with a melancholy air. Then he shook himself and walked up the path towards me with the slow flat-footed, resigned walk of a teddy bear who knows he is no longer favourite of the nursery. He approached me in this dispirited manner, his eyes blank, obviously thinking deep and morbid thoughts. I was standing quite still, and so it wasn't until he was within a couple of yards of my feet that he noticed me. To my astonishment he did not rush off into the forest— he did not even check in his advance. He walked straight up to my legs and proceeded to examine my trousers and shoes with a faintly interested air. Then he sneezed again, uttered a heartrending sigh, pushed past me unceremoniously, and continued up the path. I followed him for some time, but eventually he left the path and waddled off into the forest, and I lost him. I asked Ira about him and she said that he had been the Grand Old Man of the forest for about ten years. He was frequently seen during the day—which was unusual in a nocturnal creature like a Wombat—and he never evinced any more interest in visitors to the forest than he had shown in me. His attitude obviously was that if a lot of ungainly human beings wanted to tramp about his forest looking at a lot of noisy birds it was all right by him, provided he was not interfered with.

All that afternoon we wandered about the forest trying to find Lyrebirds in a suitable area for photography, but without success. We saw quite a number of them, but they were all lurking in the dimmest recesses of the forest. We returned to the hotel irritated, cold and hungry. On the following morning—a Sunday—the weather had lifted slightly and so we set off into the forest in high hopes. Ira, however, dampened these slightly by telling us that Sunday was a favourite day for people to visit the sanctuary and so the birds might be more disturbed than usual. She was still insistent that Old Spotty would be the best bird to concentrate on, so we made our way to the best of his dancing halls we had found, which was situated in a clearing in the forest and set in waist-high undergrowth. If he would only decide to use this particular hall that day it would be perfect for photography. It seemed as if our plan of campaign might work, for no sooner had we settled down near the dance hall than Old Spotty appeared. However, having appeared, he did absolutely nothing except stand stock still and stare at us with a vacuous expression for some minutes before disappearing into the forest again. Six times he did this during the morning, and each time we would seize the equipment and stand at the ready, quivering like

terriers at a rat hole, but to no avail. The seventh time he joined us he walked right up to us, and condescended to eat some cheese, but at the mere suggestion that he should do a display for us he stalked away. We waited patiently while a file of sightseers passed us on the path—elderly ladies, young couples and groups of boy scouts, all on their way into the forest to try to witness the Lyrebird's display. It was enchanting to think that such a sanctuary existed where so many town dwellers could come to picnic and get within a few feet to watch one of the most extraordinary of all bird displays. They came trooping past us with their packets of sandwiches and Box Brownies, and they all wished us good morning and asked us for the latest news as to where the birds were displaying. We said, rather acrimoniously, that we wished we knew. We waited and waited and there was still no sign of Spotty. Presently there was a crackling in the forest and an elderly clergyman burst into view, clasping a bulging haversack and wearing a rather battered panama. He paused when he saw us, adjusted his rimless glasses, beamed benignly and then tiptoed forward to examine our yards of coiling cable, our recording machines and the cameras, gleaming and inimical, perched like Martian monsters on their tripods.

'Are you trying to film Lyrebirds?' he enquired of our dispirited group.

'Yes,' we replied, overawed at his perspicacity.

'But there are lots down there in the forest,' he said, with a wild gesture, '*lots* of them . . . I can't remember having seen so many. That's where you should really be . . . down there.'

When he had passed on, having done his good deed for the day, Jim sighed deeply.

'If another Lyrebird comes within range I shall personally wring its neck,' he said, and added, 'and that goes for clergymen as well.'

Another hour passed. Chris by now was pacing up and down looking like the Duke of Wellington on the eve of Waterloo, when suddenly two things happened almost simultaneously. There was a burst of Lyrebird song from the forest some three or four hundred yards away, and with a muttered curse Jim leapt to his feet and, grabbing one of the cameras, bounded off into the forest. Hardly had he disappeared than Old Spotty suddenly materialised and made his way determinedly towards his dancing hall.

'Quick, quick,' said Chris in agony, grabbing the spare camera, 'you'll have to do the sound recording.'

He rushed through the undergrowth to the edge of the dancing hall and started frantically setting up the camera, while I, enveloped in yards of trailing wires, followed him. More by luck than good management, we managed to get set up before Spotty reached us. We were within six feet of the mound, which was the nearest we felt it was safe to go without disturbing the bird. Chris pressed the button, the camera started whirring, and then, as if he had been waiting for this as his cue, the fern fronds parted and Old Spotty stepped into the dancing hall. He paused to give us a regal look and then stepped up on to the leafmould stage and began his act.

I had expected something spectacular, but Old Spotty's display was so fabulous that I had great difficulty in concentrating on the job of recording. He gave a couple of preliminary, flute-like calls to get his voice in trim, and then he slightly lowered his wings, arched his tail right over his back in a shimmering white waterfall of feathers, threw back his head and from his throat poured forth a song that was almost beyond description for purity and virtuosity. Apart from trills and flutings and rich deep contralto warbles, I could recognise incorporated into the song the harsh, chattering laughter of a Kookaburra, the sounds of a Whip Bird (like the whistle and crack of a stock whip), and a sound that could only be compared with a tin can full of pebbles being rolled down a rocky slope. Funnily enough, as I say, these odd and unmelodious sounds were incorporated into the basic song so cunningly that they enhanced it rather than spoilt it. I had rather cleverly (I thought) hung the microphone within

a yard or so of where Old Spotty was singing, but when I
looked at the recording machine, I found to my horror that
it was in danger of bursting at the seams with the volume of
sound that was being poured into the microphone. I made
wild gestures at Chris to try to explain my predicament. I
could not speak to him for fear that my voice would be
picked up on the soundtrack. It was imperative—I gestured
furiously—that the microphone be moved back a bit. Chris,
darting a horrified glance at the dancing volume needle on the
recorder, nodded. Now two problems beset me: I had to
shift the microphone without disturbing Old Spotty, and in
so doing I would get into direct range of the camera unless I
crawled, Red Indian fashion, under it. I cautiously lowered
myself on to my stomach and edged forward over an area
of ground on which had been congregated—for my especial
benefit—all the spikiest bits of undergrowth in Australia. I
need not have worried about Spotty's reaction. Absorbed

and enamoured of his own performance as any actor, he would, I think, have allowed me to pull his tail-feathers out without even noticing, but on the off-chance that he might have come out of his Narcissus-like trance and ceased his display, I had to retrieve the microphone in slow motion. It was at this point that I discovered one of the basic truths of life, that a thorn driven into your flesh in slow motion is infinitely more painful than a thorn driven in rapidly. Eventually, however, I managed to get the microphone back to a position where it was not in danger of disintegrating with the volume of Spotty's song. Chris and I, crouched in our ungainly positions, stood there for about a quarter of an hour while Spotty poured his soul out. He ended on a gorgeous contralto trill and then, lowering his tail and shuffling his wings once or twice, he stalked out of his dancing hall and into the undergrowth.

Chris turned and stared at me with the slightly wide-eyed,

incredulous expression that always spreads over his face when things have gone right. He summed it up with his normal masterly command of understatement. 'I think that's okay,' he said.

Plucking a large amount of Australian undergrowth from the regions immediately surrounding my umbilical, I rose to my feet and surveyed him with interest.

'Yes, I think it will be okay,' I said. 'Of course, it would have been much better if we could have put him under contract and taken him to Bristol to repeat the whole thing in the studio.'

Chris gave me a withering look and we packed up the equipment and made our way back to the ride.

'Did you get anything?' Jacquie enquired anxiously.

'Well, we got something,' said Chris, with his air of an elder statesman who does not want to confess that neither he nor his party knows what his policy is, 'but whether it will turn out all right or not remains to be seen.'

'It was a very dicey piece of work,' I said to Jacquie, 'and the dice were loaded against us. The only thing in our favour was that we were within four feet of a mentally defective Lyrebird who was going through his full display, and short of actually pushing the microphone down into his crop, we couldn't have got any closer, but as far as Parsons is concerned, this constitutes a rather hit and miss type of natural history filming.'

Chris looked at me malevolently but his retort was cut short by the reappearance of Jim, who sauntered out of the undergrowth whistling happily but unmusically to himself. Beaming at us all impartially, he laid the camera on the ground and patted it affectionately. 'Every one a little Rembrandt,' he said, 'you've no need to worry, Chris . . . it's in the bag . . . I've got the lot . . . trust Jim.'

'What have you got?' enquired Chris, suspiciously.

'All the inner secrets of a Lyrebird's life,' said Jim airily. 'There they were, galloping to and fro, stamping their feet and carrying on like mad things. I've never seen anything like it since I was at that Palais de Danse in Slough.'

'What did you get?' said Chris trenchantly.

'I've just told you,' said Jim, 'everything. Lyrebirds galloping about shaking their tails at each other, the lot. While you were all mucking about here, I just nipped off into the undergrowth and got it. Saved the series, I have. Still, we can always share the Television Award between us.'

It was quite some time before we could get Jim to tell us simply and concisely what, in fact, he had got, which turned out to be one of the best bits of film that were taken on the trip.

Irritated by the lack of co-operation on the part of the Lyrebirds, he had plunged off into the undergrowth when he had heard them calling, and had come upon a scene which very few people witness, let alone are able to film. In a valley with sufficient light for photography to be possible, he had discovered a cock Lyrebird who had wandered over the strict demarcation line into the territory of another cock bird. The result had been something quite spectacular. The owner of the territory had cast his mist-like tail over his head and stamped forward to do battle, lurching from side to side, stamping his feet and bobbing his head. The whole thing looked like a Red Indian war dance. The other bird knew that he was intruding but, in order to save face, he had to put up some sort of aggressive show, so he, too, cast his tail over his head and proceeded to stamp and sway. Both birds were uttering loud, ringing and doubtless derisive cries at each other as they did this. With their tails practically obscuring their bodies, they looked like glittering, animated waterfalls on legs, and the rustling of their tail-feathers was like the sound of wind among autumn leaves. Eventually, honour having been satisfied, the intruding Lyrebird retreated and Jim had come back to us in a state of jubilation. So, in spite of being incessantly rained upon and being subjected to the coldest weather I have experienced outside Patagonia, we had been successful in filming the Lyrebirds.

The next task we had to tackle was to try to film Leadbeater's Possum. This is a small and rather enchanting animal that had quite suddenly disappeared—or so it seemed—from the face of the earth. It had originally been discovered in 1894 and was known from several museum skins; then it vanished and everyone was convinced that, as its range appeared to be limited, it had become extinct. In 1948, to the astonishment of incredulous naturalists, a tiny pocket of Leadbeater's Possum was discovered in the eucalyptus forest not far from Melbourne. The exact location was kept a secret, for fear that crowds of well-meaning naturalists and sightseers would troop up there and disturb the terrain.

Quite naturally, therefore, when I mentioned to Mr. Butcher that we would very much like to film Leadbeater's Possum, he gave me a look in which suspicion and commiseration were nicely blended. He explained that, although they knew the location of the Leadbeater's Possum, they knew nothing about the extent of its habitat nor, indeed, the number of individual animals that inhabited the area, and therefore we might go tramping about the forest for weeks on end without catching a glimpse of one. With the cold dampness of Sherbrooke Forest still lurking in the marrow of my bones, I smiled bravely and said this did not matter, provided we had the faintest chance of seeing this elusive marsupial. I added that of course we would still keep the exact location secret, but if we could get some shots of the Possum, it would

be a tremendous achievement for us and would aid in the
conservation story that we were endeavouring to tell on film.
We were quite prepared, I said (lavishly condemning Jacquie,
Chris and Jim), to tramp about the forest for nights on end
in order to try to catch a glimpse of Leadbeater's Possum, if
only Mr. Butcher would unlock his lips and vouchsafe to us
the exact location.

Impressed, either by my imbecility or my devotion to duty,
or both, Mr. Butcher sighed lugubriously and said that he
could arrange to send us out to Leadbeater's Possum country,
guided by one of the young scientists who had actually re-
discovered the creature, but he could not guarantee what
results we would get. However, just in case we were dis-
appointed, he said, if I cared to follow him, he had something
to show me. Whereupon he took me down to the large
Wildlife laboratory, full of spirit specimens, charts, diagrams
and other accoutrements of a scientist's trade, and led me to a
small, upright cage, not unlike a cupboard with a wire door.
Opening it, he thrust his hand into a small sleeping box inside
and produced, to my incredulous astonishment, a pair of
wide-eyed, fat and exceedingly friendly Leadbeater's Possums.

It was as incredible and as thrilling as suddenly being presented with a pair of live Dodos or a baby Dinosaur. They
crouched, soft as velvet, in my cupped hands, peering up at me,
their noses and ears twitching, their big, dark eyes still slightly
bleary from having been extracted from a pleasant siesta so
unceremoniously. They were about the size of a Bushbaby,
with sleek, soft, mole-like fur, handsomely patterned in ash
grey, white and black, the hair on their busy tails so fine that
it looked like spun glass. They had rather squat, fat, good-
natured looking faces, and tiny, delicate paws. When they
had recovered consciousness to a certain extent, they sat up on
their hind legs in my hands, portly and sedate, and accepted

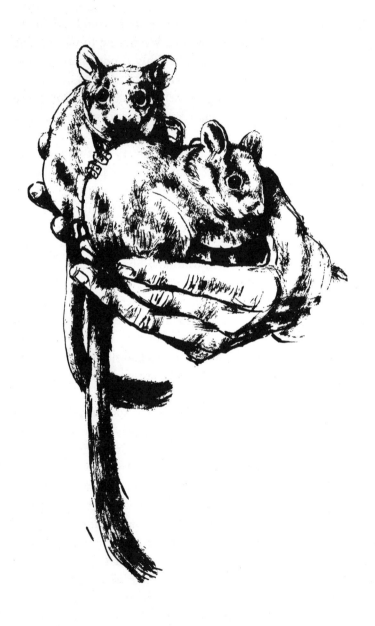

a couple of mealworms with an air of condescension. Mr. Butcher explained that, having rediscovered these charming little creatures, they thought it would be advisable to capture a pair and try to establish them in captivity in case anything untoward happened to the colony. After we had gloated over the enchanting little marsupials for some time we took pity on them and returned them to their bedroom to continue their interrupted sleep. Then Mr. Butcher introduced us to Bob Wanerke, a handsome young Australian who seemed about seven feet tall and as wide as a barn door. Bob had been doing some studies on the Leadbeater's Possum, and he said he would be delighted to lead us to their last stronghold, although he did not guarantee that we would see any. We said that we quite understood, as we had had similar experiences before.

The night was moonless and bitterly cold when Bob appeared to lead us to the Leadbeaters. The four of us sat huddled in the Land-Rover, wearing every stitch of clothing we could find, and still our teeth were chattering. We followed Bob's vehicle out of Melbourne and for some time we drove through fairly open country; then the road started to climb and we entered deep, tall eucalyptus forest, the tree trunks looking even more weirdly distorted than normal in our headlights. As we climbed higher and higher it became colder and colder.

'Come to sunny Australia,' mused Jim, 'that's what they say. The country that's ninety in the shade and where everyone has a suntan. All a load of old codswallop.'

'I must say that is rather the impression you get in England,' I agreed. 'I never thought it would be as cold as this.'

'What we want are a few hot-water bottles or a warming-pan or something,' said Jacquie, her voice muffled from the depths of her sheepskin jacket.

There was a short silence while I tried to remember if I had packed a bottle of Scotch.

'I once,' said Jim reminiscently, 'set fire to a bed with a hair drier.'

We absorbed this item of information in silence, each of us trying to imagine how even Jim could have achieved such a task. At length we gave up the unequal struggle.

'Well?' I enquired.

'It was when I first got married. My wife and I were living in a furnished room. The landlady was a real old female dog—you know the sort: couldn't do this and couldn't do that; scared the pants off me, she did. Well, it was damned cold then and the only way we had of warming the bed was my wife's hair drier. Worked a treat, I can tell you. You put a couple of pillows on each side, hair drier in the middle, pull the clothes up and Bob's your uncle, you've got a lovely warm bed in half an hour.'

Jim paused and sighed lugubriously.

'Then one night,' he continued, 'something went wrong. Before we knew what was happening, whoosh! Whole bed on fire. Flames, clouds of smoke, feathers everywhere. We were more frightened of the landlady than anything else, in case she found out and threw us into the street in the middle of the night. I'd thrown water on the bed to put the fire out and this contributed to the mess. Took us half the night to clean it up and we spent the rest of the night in chairs. Next day I had to smuggle the mattress out and buy a new one. Never again. Hot-water bottles for me now.'

We were now quite high up in the hills, deep in the eucalyptus forest and a number of miles from Melbourne. Presently Bob's vehicle ahead of us turned off the main road and headed down a rough track that seemed to lead into the heart of the forest, but after a couple of hundred yards we came to a clearing in which was a tiny hut. Here we stopped and disgorged ourselves and our equipment. Bob had brought a number of hunting lights with him (the sort that you strap to your head and that work from a battery slung at your waist) and these we now put on. Then, when the rest of the equipment was ready, we set off in single file down the rough track into the forest. We walked slowly and quietly, stopping every now and then to listen, flashing our headlights all around us. The silence was complete. It was as though all the eucalyptus trees the moment before had been performing a wild, abandoned dance, and had frozen suspiciously into immobility at our appearance. You could have heard a pin drop; the only sound was the faint scruff of our shoes in the leaves. We walked on for a quarter of a mile or so in this uncanny silence: we might have been in a cave in the depths of the earth, with the eucalyptus trees like weird stalagmites sprouting up around us. Presently Bob came to a standstill and beckoned me.

'From here onwards for about a mile is the area where we generally see them,' he whispered, and then added depressingly, '*if* we do.'

We moved slowly on and we hadn't gone many yards when Bob suddenly froze and shone his light at the forest floor some twenty feet away. We stood quite still and held our breath. From the bushes ahead we could hear a faint rustling, the tiniest whisper of sound. Bob stood quite still, flashing his light to and fro like a lighthouse. For some time nothing happened and the rustling went on, then suddenly, in his torch beam, appeared one of the weirdest-looking little animals it has been my privilege to meet. It was about the size of a rabbit with an elongated, whiffling nose, bright beady eyes and pointed, pixie-like ears. It was clad in rather coarse looking, yellowing-brown fur and it had a rather rat-like

147

tail. It pottered through the fallen leaves, its nose working overtime, pausing now and then to scratch with its neat little feet in the leafmould, presumably in search of insects.

'What is it?' whispered Jacquie.

'It's a Long-Nosed Bandicoot,' I whispered back.

'Don't be facetious,' she hissed, 'I want to *know*.'

'I can't help its name,' I whispered irritably, 'that's what they're called.'

The Long-Nosed Bandicoot, oblivious of my wife's disbelief, was now walking through a drift of fallen leaves, ploughing them up with his nose, like a curiously shaped bulldozer; then he sat down suddenly and scratched himself with great vigour and concentration for a moment or so. This relaxing occupation completed, he sat in a sort of trance for a few seconds, sneezed violently and suddenly, and then bull-dozed his way off into the undergrowth.

We drifted on for a few hundred yards and came eventually

to a clearing among the great trees, and here we got our second indication that the forest was not as lifeless as it seemed. Standing in the clearing we shone our lights up at the topmost foliage of some giant eucalyptus trees and suddenly, in our torch beams, four eyes gleamed like gigantic rubies. Moving slowly round to a better vantage point, we saw the animals to which the eyes belonged. They looked, at first sight, like a pair of huge black squirrels with long, smoothly furred tails: they were half in and half out of a hole in the trunk where a great branch had been ripped away and left a hollow. Disturbed by the lights, they moved out of the hollow and made their way along a branch and this enabled us to see them more clearly. They really were only squirrel-like in shape—there the resemblance ended. They had furry, rather leaf-shaped ears, and round, vaguely cat-like faces with little boot-button noses; you could see along the sides of the body a loose flap of skin now, as they were sitting, folded along their ribs in scallops like a curtain. I knew they were Possums of some sort but I could not place them.

'What are they?' I whispered to Bob.

'Greater Glider Possums,' he whispered back. 'They're the largest of the Glider Possums—they're fairly common up here. Wait, and I'll try and make them fly.'

He picked up a stick and approached the trunk of the tree. The Possums watched him with interest. Reaching the base of the tree, Bob hit the trunk a couple of mighty whacks with his branch, and immediately the Possums' air of benevolent interest changed to one of panic. They ran to and fro along their branch, chittering to each other like a couple of spinsters who have found a man under the bed. The fact that they were some seventy feet above Bob and quite safe did not appear to occur to them. Bob belaboured the trunk of the tree and the Possums grew more and more panicky; then one of them—

uttering a cat-like mew—launched himself off the branch into the air. As he left the branch he stretched out his arms and legs to their fullest extent and, as the flaps of skin along the side of his body became taut to act as 'wings', he assumed a sort of shoe-box shape, with a head at one end and his long tail streaming out at the other. Silently banking and weaving with uncanny, glider-like skill, he skimmed over the clearing and came to rest on a tree trunk some eighty feet away, with all the ease of an expertly made paper dart. The other one soon followed him, drifting and banking through the air, and eventually landed on the same tree, only a bit lower down. Once they were reunited they both humped themselves up the trunk and disappeared into the thick foliage at the top of the tree. I had been very impressed by the flight of these lovely creatures, particularly by the distance they had covered, but Bob told me that this was a comparatively short glide: they had been known to cover 120 yards in one glide and in six successive glides to cover 590 yards.

Although the creatures we had seen so far were fascinating, we still had not caught up with our main quarry, so we pressed on into the forest. We had been moving so slowly and meandering through the undergrowth with our lights that we felt we had been walking for miles, whereas in reality we were only about a quarter of a mile from our starting point. We had one false alarm when we saw a Lesser Glider up in a tree; in size and shape it looked, in the torchlight, just like a Leadbeater's Possum, but it proved its identity for us by launching itself into the air and floating away through the branches like a flake of wood ash. It was getting on for one o'clock now and the cold was so intense that I felt as if both my feet and hands had been amputated at the wrist and ankle. I was thinking longing thoughts of log fires and hot whisky, when Bob came to a standstill and shone his torch beam into some low eucalyptus scrub ahead of us, then took three quick steps to the right, and from this new vantage point raked the foliage with his beam. Suddenly his light centred on one particular spot and there, sitting on a branch some twelve feet away, fat, furry and completely unconcerned, was a Leadbeater's Possum.

Although I had already seen the live ones in the Wildlife Department's laboratory at Melbourne, it did not detract in any way from the thrill of seeing that rare little marsupial squatting among the eucalyptus leaves in its native forest. I kept my torch beam steadily on him and drank in every detail. He was sitting sideways on to us, blinking his large dark eyes as if in mild expostulation at the brightness of our torches; after a moment he attempted to sit up on the branch and give his whiskers a combing, but the branch was too narrow to allow such a manœuvre and he fell off, only saving himself in the nick of time with his front paws. He clung there, struggling to get his hind limbs back on to the branch, looking like a portly and very amateur trapeze artist who has only just made the trapeze. Eventually he managed to haul himself back, and after a short pause to regain his breath he ambled slowly down the branch in a preoccupied sort of way; then, without warning and with a speed and agility extraordinary for one of his rotundity, he leapt to another branch some six feet away, landing as softly as thistledown. Here, to our delight, he was joined by what appeared to be his mate. She came running out of the leaves and they greeted each other in a series of tiny, breathless squeaks. Then the new arrival squatted on the branch and proceeded to comb the fur of her mate, while he sat there looking exceedingly smug. They seemed completely unconcerned by both the lights and our whispered conversation, but at that moment I moved rather incautiously and trod on a stick that broke with a report like a small cannon going off. The two Possums froze in the middle of a passionate embrace and then, like lightning, they turned and in three graceful jumps they had disappeared into the gloom of the forest. I cursed my stupidity, but comforted myself with the thought that we had been incredibly lucky to see these rare little creatures at all, let alone spend ten minutes looking in on their private lives. We made our way back to the clearing where we had left the cars, and went into the little hut. Here we soon kindled a roaring and aromatic fire of eucalyptus wood, and sat round it, thawing ourselves out with the aid of hot whisky and water, heavily laced with sugar. Then, when our bodies once more belonged to us and we were glowing with heat, we climbed into the Land-Rovers and started on the long drive back to Melbourne. It had been an evening I would not have missed for the world.

CHAPTER 5

A Treeful of Bears

'His form is ungainly—his intellect small—'
(So the Bellman would often remark).
Hunting of the Snark

THE TEMPERATURE IN THE CAB of the Land-Rover was soaring somewhere in the nineties, and we were hot, dusty and tired, having driven up from Melbourne, through New South Wales and over the border into Queensland. The contrast between these blue and cloudless skies and fierce sun compared with the freezing drizzle we had been subjected to in Melbourne was most marked. However, none of us dared complain, for only twenty-four hours previously we had been cursing the cold and praying for sunshine. Now we had it in abundance, and the sweat trickled lavishly down our faces. Presently the road curved gently down into a valley filled with rustling, pink-trunked eucalyptus trees, and by the side of the road was a neat notice-board on which was printed

DRIVE CAREFULLY
KOALAS CROSS HERE AT NIGHT

I knew then that we were getting close to our objective, David Fleay's Fauna Reserve at Barren Pines.

David Fleay is probably one of Australia's best-known naturalists. For years he has kept and written about the fascinating fauna of Australia, and, among other things, was the first man to breed the Duck-Billed Platypus in captivity. For years I had known of David Fleay's work and he was one of the people I most wanted to meet in Australia; for many years he had been in charge of the Healsville Sanctuary in Victoria, but recently he had left there and moved up to Queensland to start his own Reserve on the Gold Coast, that strip of sunlit beaches that is the Australian Riviera. Half an hour's drive and three Koala Crossing signs later we came to a pleasant house tucked away on a hillside overlooking a valley filled with eucalyptus trees and shrubs and plants ablaze with multicoloured, sub-tropical flowers. We rang a convenient bell and waited dutifully, and presently David Fleay appeared.

If anybody could be said to look 'typically' Australian, then it is definitely David Fleay. He is the personification of what everyone thinks an Australian *ought* to look like, but so seldom does. Over six feet in height, he was well built but not over muscular—whipcord rather than weightlifter. His face was weatherbeaten and wind-wrinkled, and his blue eyes were gentle, tolerant and shrewd, with a perpetual twinkle lurking in their depths. To complete the picture of the typical Aussie, he was wearing a Stetson-type hat and looked as though he had just wandered in from some mysterious foray into the outback. He greeted us with warm enthusiasm and with a certain diffidence which was charming; so many people, when they reach David's eminence, are apt to have a far better opinion of themselves than their achievements warrant, but David was so modest and self-effacing that it was a pleasure to talk to him. He never boasted about his own achievements but gave all the credit to his animals, for they, as far as he was concerned, were the most important things in life. Apart from breeding the Platypus, itself no mean achievement, David has kept and bred more of the smaller and rarer Australian

marsupials than anyone else in the world, and so his knowledge is vast.

A lot of David's animals—the kangaroos, wallabies, Emus and so on—were kept in spacious paddocks and the visitors could enter these through self-closing doors. Thus the public were, so to speak, caged with the animals, which was an excellent idea, for it allowed them to get on much more intimate terms with the creatures they had come to see. Collecting a large bucketful of bread crusts, David took me down to the largest of the paddocks, which housed a mixed collection of kangaroos, wallabies, ibis and a young Cassowary named Claude. He stood about three feet high and was clad in hair-like plumage which looked as though he never preened it—he looked, to be perfectly candid, like a badly made feather duster   He had thick, ostrich-like legs, a Donald Duck beak and a wild and determined eye: in spite of the fact that he was considerably smaller than the kangaroos and wallabies whose paddock he shared, there was no doubt at all as to who was the boss.   David and I sat on a fallen tree trunk and started to distribute our largesse, and in a moment we were surrounded by a milling mob of kangaroos and wallabies, all nuzzling eagerly but gently at our hands to get the bread crusts.   Claude had been standing at the far end of the paddock, meditating—to judge by his expression—on the sins of the world, and he suddenly woke up to the fact that there was a free meal going which he was in danger of missing. He came out of his trance with a jerk and ran towards us with a loping stride, his big feet thumping the ground;   arriving at the outskirts of the mob of marsupials around us, he proceeded to fight his way to the front row by the simple process of kicking every kangaroo and wallaby backside in sight.   They were obviously used to this form of attack and were quite adroit at hopping out of the way at the crucial moment, and at one point, when Claude decided to use both feet to kick a large Grey Kangaroo out of the way, the kangaroo (in a very cowardly fashion) hopped to one side and Claude fell flat on his back.   He got to his feet, his eyes blazing, and waded into the crowd of marsupials with such vigour that they all scattered before him like sheep before a sheep dog.   Any one of the bigger kangaroos could have killed Claude with one well-directed kick, but they were too well-mannered to attempt this.   Having driven off all the competition Claude came back to us and proceeded to engulf bread crusts with a speed that had to be seen to be believed. Presently the kangaroos and wallabies started to drift back again, and Claude had to keep interrupting his gluttony in order to chase them away.   When Claude was fully grown he would measure some five feet in height, and I could not help thinking that if he persisted in his belligerent attitude to other creatures it would be safer—when he reached manhood —to give him a paddock on his own.

In the next enclosure was David's group of Emus—large, slow-moving and wearing the most vacuous and self-satisfied expressions. Among them was a white one with pale gentian blue eyes, who was busy sitting on a nest of four eggs. The marital life of an Emu is one that would delight the most militant of suffragettes: having enjoyed all the pleasures of the nuptial couch (as it were) the female then lays her eggs and forgets about the whole sordid business. It is the male who constructs the nest (if it can be dignified with that term), collects the eggs, sits on them devotedly—without food— until they hatch out, and then takes charge of the youngsters and looks after them until they are old enough to fend for themselves. Meanwhile the females are simply disporting themselves in the eucalyptus groves, the ultimate in emancipation.

I wanted to see the eggs that the White Emu was incubating so assiduously, and David told me to go into the paddock and push him off the nest, as he was perfectly tame and would not take exception to this. Until I tried it I had never realised how difficult it is to remove a reluctant Emu from its nest. To begin with it seems to weigh about a ton, and secondly there does not appear to be any part of its anatomy on which you can get a firm grip. He just sat there phlegmatically while I struggled with his ungainly body and achieved nothing more than the dislodging of several handfuls of feathers. At last, by getting my knee under his breast and using it as a lever, I raised him to his feet and managed to push him back from the nest; then I hastily crouched over the nest, as though I was brooding the eggs, to prevent him from returning. The Emu stood just behind me, staring down at me thoughtfully. In spite of the fact that David had assured me he was tame, I still kept a close eye on him, for a well-placed kick from an Emu could easily kill one, and I can't imagine a more *infra dig* way for a naturalist to die than to be kicked to death by a bird.

The eggs looked as though they were made of terracotta and were some six inches long, in a very beautiful shade of dark olive green, with a sort of raised pattern all over the shell, like a bas relief. While I had been concentrating on the eggs I had, momentarily, forgotten the rightful owner of the nest, so it came as something of a shock to realise that he had seized this opportunity to creep up on me. I suddenly felt him spreading his great, feathery bulk over my back, almost precipitating me into the nest on top of the eggs; he laid his

long neck over my shoulder and then, twisting his head round, peered into my face benignly from a distance of about six inches, at the same time producing a sound deep inside his breast that sounded like a mad tap-dancer in a pair of army boots covorting on a bass drum. Not being quite sure how to cope with these advances I just stared into the bird's hypnotic blue eyes and did nothing. He had now twisted his head almost upside down, presumably to see if my face looked more attractive this way up. He gave another burst of drumming and then, digging his feet into the ground, pushed me inexorably towards the nest—I felt that the implication was that I should share with him his labour of love, but I had better things to do than squat on a lot of Emu eggs. Slowly, so as not to give offence, I rose to my feet and retreated. The Emu watched me go sadly; his expression implied that he had hoped of better things from me. Then he stood up, shuffled his feathers with a sound like an oak tree in a summer breeze, stepped forward to the nest and lowered himself delicately on to his precious eggs.

When I had recovered from my amorous interlude with the Emu, David took me to see some specimens of which he was —quite rightly—inordinately proud: it was his breeding colony of Taipan, Australia's deadliest snake. Just simply keeping some snakes in captivity is difficult, and to keep them and breed them is a great achievement, but to have kept and bred something as rare and shy as a Taipan is a very great triumph. They are the third largest poisonous snake in the world (only being beaten by the King Cobra and the Black Mamba) and can grow to a length of eleven feet; a large one can produce as much as three hundred milligrammes of poison, an unpleasant dose to have injected into your bloodstream should you be bitten. It is twice as much venom as is produced by any other poisonous Australian snake, and is pumped into you with the aid of half-inch long fangs.

David's group were lolling about elegantly in their well appointed cage, and they really looked wonderful. Their bodies were a rich, burnished copper, so that they looked as if they had been newly polished; their underparts were a sort of iridescent mother-of-pearl, and their faces a pale, biscuit brown. They had very slender necks and large lustrous eyes and they looked what they were: beautiful and deadly. David told me of the exciting hunts he had been on to capture these snakes—hunts which were not only exciting but dangerous as well, for a Taipan has been known to kill a horse in five minutes with a well-aimed bite. He showed me Alexandra, a slim and beautiful seven footer, who was the proud mother that had regularly laid twenty eggs each year. David removed the eggs and kept them in a special incubator where, after a hundred and seven days of incubation, they finally hatched. The remarkable thing was that the eggs measured two and a half inches by one and a half, and yet the babies that hatched out from them measured fifteen inches long: Taipans are obviously adept at getting a quart into a pint pot. David regularly 'milks' his snakes of their venom, and this is then sent to the Commonwealth Serum Laboratory to be made into Taipan anti-venom, which has already saved the lives of a number of people who have had the misfortune to be bitten. This 'milking' is done by covering a glass or some similar receptacle with a piece of gauze. The snake is then caught, its mouth opened, and the fangs are sunk through the gauze. The poison then drips into the glass container.

At that moment the bell outside the house clanged imperiously and two Brolgas, or Native Cranes, in a paddock nearby spread their wings and started a wild dance, pointing their beaks to the sky and trumpeting like mad.

'Tea's ready,' said David laconically. 'They always dance

when they hear the bell. Very useful if you want to photo-graph them.'

The Brolgas continued their mad dance while we drank our tea and watched them. They were handsome birds, a soft slate grey with a vivid red and yellow marking on the head. Like most cranes they were consummate dancers and pranced and pirouetted and bowed in the most dainty manner; in the wild state they will sometimes gather together in great groups and hold a sort of avian ball, waltzing and prancing with each other under the blue skies, a sight which—according to many people—is one of the most extraordinary things you can see in Australia.

After tea, David took us to see the animal for which he is most famous; the unbelievable Duck-Billed Platypus. Although the Platypus has been written up *ad nauseam*, it *is* such an incredible creature that it's worth running over its more startling features once again. The rubbery beak and the webbed feet are like a duck's; the body is covered with a short and exceedingly soft fur like that of a mole; the short, some-what paddle-shaped tail resembles that of a beaver; on the hind legs the male is armed with spurs that contain a poison almost as virulent as that of a snake; finally, as if all that was not enough, it is a mammal (which means that it is warm-blooded and suckles its young on milk) but the young are hatched out of eggs. The Platypus, incidentally, has no teats like a normal mammal, but merely an area of spongy skin through which it exudes the milk which the young ones then lap up. It is a strictly insectivorous creature, feeding on fresh-water crayfish, worms and grubs, and consuming its own weight in these delicacies each night. It is this prodigious appetite that is one of the many reasons that Platypus are so difficult to keep in captivity.

David's pair were housed in his specially designed Platypusary. This was a large, shallow pond, at one end of which were the wooden sleeping quarters—shallow boxes filled with hay connected to the pond by long wooden tunnels lined with Sorbo rubber. The reason for this is that in the wild state the Platypus burrows are narrow, and when the animal wends its way up the burrow to its bedroom the surplus moisture in its fur is squeezed out by contact with the walls of the burrow: in captivity, David has found that it is best to line the tunnels with hay or Sorbo rubber, which will perform the same function, for should a Platypus reach his bedroom with his fur still damp he will almost inevitably catch a chill and die. The Platypuses were not in their pond when we arrived at the Platypusary, so David obligingly opened up a bedroom, plunged his hand into the crisp hay bed, and pulled one out for our inspection.

Now, although I had never seen a live Platypus, I had, over the years, seen films and photographs of them; I knew about their curious anatomy, how many eggs they lay, what they feed on, and so on. In fact I felt I knew the Platypus fairly well, but as I gazed at the creature wriggling in David's hands I suddenly realised that all my study of the Platypus over the years had left me completely unprepared for one thing: the personality of the beast. The curve of the beak gave it a benign and perpetual smile, and its round, brown, boot-button eyes gleamed with personality. It looked, quite frankly, like one of Donald Duck's nicer relatives clad in a fur coat some three sizes too large for it. You almost expected it to quack and in fact the noise it did make resembled the disgruntled growl of an indignant broody hen. David placed the Platypus on the ground and it waddled about eagerly, with movements reminiscent of a baby otter, snuffling interestedly at every object it came across.

David has not only kept and bred the Platypus in captivity

(the first man to do so) but he has twice undertaken the hazardous task of accompanying Platypus to the New York Zoological Society. When you consider the organisation involved in such a venture, the mind boggles: the thousands of worms, crayfish and frogs to be obtained for the journey; the special Platypusary that has to be built; the slow and careful conditioning of the animals to prepare them for the trip, for Platypuses are immensely highly strung and any upset can make them go off their food and die. It says much for David's abilities and patience that on both occasions he landed his charges alive and well, and they lived successfully for a number of years in the United States.

'You know, there was a very odd rumour circulating in England during the war,' I said to David, 'It was about 1942, if I remember right. Someone told me that a Platypus was being sent to the London Zoo, but I heard no more about it, so I suppose it was only a rumour. Do you know anything about it?'

'That wasn't a rumour,' said David grinning, 'that was a fact.'

'What,' I asked in astonishment, 'ferrying Platypus about in the middle of a world war?'

'Yes,' said David, 'sounds a bit mad, doesn't it? Suddenly, in the middle of the war, Winston Churchill decided that he wanted a Platypus. Whether he thought it would be good for morale, or a good propaganda story, or whether he just wanted a Platypus, I don't know; anyway, I was approached by Menzies and given the job of catching the animal, getting it used to captivity and preparing it for the voyage. Well, I got a nice young male and after keeping him for six months I thought he was about ready for the voyage. I'd briefed an apprentice on the ship about keeping the animal, and given him masses of written instructions as well. The whole ship was intensely interested in the scheme and I got wonderful co-operation, so eventually the Platypus sailed on the *Port Phillip*.'

David paused and gazed thoughtfully down at the Platypus, which was endeavouring to eat his shoe; then he bent and picked it up carefully by its tail and slid it into its bedroom.

'Do you know,' he continued, 'they got that Platypus right across the Pacific, through the Panama Canal, across the Atlantic and then—two days out from Liverpool—there was a submarine alert. Well, they had to drop depth charges, of course. As I told you, a Platypus is highly temperamental and very susceptible to noise; the depth charges exploding were the last straw as far as the animal was concerned, and it just died. Two days out from Liverpool!'

To me the whole story was one of the most gloriously Quixotic things I had ever heard. Humanity being torn asunder by the most terrible war in history, and in the middle of it Churchill, with his cigar, trenchantly demanding a Platypus (of all things), and on the other side of the world David carefully and patiently training a young Platypus and preparing it for the long voyage through submarine-infested waters. What a pity the story did not have a happy ending. But, even so, what a magnificently idiotic thing to do at that time. I doubt whether Hitler, even in his saner moments, would have ever had the delightful eccentricity of mind to ask for a Duck-Billed Platypus in the middle of the war.

After three days spent filming in the charming company of David and his wife, we reluctantly had to pack up our gear and move down south again to Melbourne. The Wildlife Department there had organised a bear hunt for us which we did not want to miss, and on the way down through New South Wales we hoped to see the Mallee-Fowl, one of Australia's more incredible birds. So we said goodbye to

David and his wife and, leaving his charming sanctuary, started on the long drive down to Melbourne.

Our first landfall was the small town of Griffith in the centre of New South Wales. Near the town lay a fair-sized area of Mallee country, and it was here we hoped to see the Mallee-Fowl. At Griffith we were met by Bevan Bowan of CSIRO (The Commonwealth Scientific and Industrial Research Organization). Under Harry Frith, the director of the Wildlife Survey section of this organisation, Bevan had been helping in a study of the breeding habits and ecology of the Mallee Fowl, and so he was to act as our guide and adviser.

Mallee scrub consists of a small species of eucalyptus between six and twenty feet high, and in places the trees grow very close together, their branches entwining and forming a continuous canopy. Although at first sight the Mallee scrub looks dead, grey, desiccated and devoid of life, it is, in reality, one of the most interesting types of country to be found in Australia, for many species of insect and bird have adapted themselves to this somewhat harsh environment and are found nowhere else. As many isolated groups of islands in the world (the Galapagos for example) have evolved their own unique species, so the Mallee scrub, spread like a string of islands over the continent, has evolved its own special fauna; but without doubt the most interesting species to inhabit the Mallee scrub is the Mallee-Fowl—a handsome, turkey-sized bird that (to borrow Harry Frith's description) builds an incubator. Unfortunately, it was not the breeding season when Bevan took us out to the Mallee scrub, but we were lucky enough to see both the incubator and its owners.

The grey-green Mallee we drove through was hot, silent and apparently lifeless. After we had driven some little distance into the scrub, Bevan pulled up and said that we would go the rest of the way on foot, as this would give us a better chance of seeing a Mallee-Fowl if there were any about. It was during this short walk that I discovered that the Mallee is not as deserted and lifeless as it appears: bronze-winged pigeons, their wings purring among the leaves, took frantic flight as we approached; tiny, slim brown lizards with golden eyes glided among the fallen leaves under our feet, and turning over a rotten log I found a small, black and extremely malevolent scorpion crouching with a misanthropic air. Digging my hand into the earth underneath the log I dredged up two extraordinary little creatures: at first sight they looked like golden snakes, some five inches long and as slender as a matchstick; it was only by looking at them closely that you noticed the four frail, rudimentary legs which fitted in grooves in the skin alongside the body. When they moved these lizards did not use their legs at all, but kept them held in to the side of their bodies and progressed as a snake does. I got quite enthusiastic over my find, but Chris was champing at the bit and eager to get to grips with the Mallee-Fowl, so I reluctantly returned the lizards to their earthy bed and we moved on.

Presently we came to a slight clearing and in the centre of it was what appeared to be a crater made by a small but vigorous bomb. The hole itself was the circumference of a small dustbin, but the earth had been thrown up around it in a wall measuring some twelve feet across. This, Bevan explained, was the incubator, and he went on to explain all the mysteries of these strange earthworks. In the winter time the cock Mallee-Fowl (sometimes aided by a hen) digs out this enormous crater and then he fills the hole in the middle with rotting vegetation and covers it carefully with sand. The rain and the sun do their work, the vegetation ferments, and soon the temperature in the interior of the incubator rises.

Then he uncovers the nest and the females come and lay their eggs, arranging them in layers in the vegetation, big end up; the cock then carefully covers them up with sand. Now if the Mallee-Fowl was a reptile, that would be the end of the job: he would simply go away and leave the eggs to be hatched out by the heat of the sun, but the Mallee-Fowl is more particular about his eggs than the average reptile, and he likes them kept at a steady 95 degrees. On the face of it you might think this was an impossible task for a bird, but the Mallee-Fowl manages very successfully. Either his tongue or the soft membrane inside his beak (no one is quite sure which as yet) acts as a built-in thermometer, and with it he can gauge the temperature in the nest with incredible accuracy. So, day after day, he tends the nest, plunging his open beak into the sand to judge the heat, and removing or adding more material as the temperature rises or falls; daily, for six or seven months, the bird watches his nest, making sure that the precious eggs are neither chilled nor cooked. His devotion to his task is extraordinary. If rain clouds appear and a storm seems to be threatening, the Mallee-Fowl will run to his nest and frantically pile the sand in a cone over the nest chamber, thus providing a sort of 'roof' off which the rain can run. Attack the nest with a shovel and try to uncover the eggs, and again the cock arrives at the double, and so great is his anxiety that he will stand next to you and shovel the sand back into the nest with his feet as fast as you uncover it. Eventually, all the bird's hard work is rewarded and the eggs hatch, but, once having escaped from the egg, the chick finds itself buried under some two feet of hot sand and has to dig its way out. This is a slow and laborious process and can take the chick anything from two to fifteen hours before he breaks through the surface. Once out of the mound the chick is extremely weak and helpless and it generally staggers away from the mound to the nearest patch of shade, where it rests and gains strength. Within two hours it is strong enough to run quite fast, and within twenty-four hours it can fly.

Soon, when we had finished examining the mound, Bevan led us deeper into the Mallee scrub in search of the birds. We quartered the scrub for about an hour without success, and were just about to give up when Bevan came to a sudden standstill and pointed. Ahead of us, in a small clearing, stood two Mallee-Fowl, regarding us suspiciously. Basically they were a soft and lovely shade of pinky-grey, but with the back, wings and tail handsomely spotted and flecked with reddish-brown, old gold and grey; from under the chin down the front of the breast was a sort of cravat of similar markings. They were far more handsome than I had imagined, and I dearly wanted to get closer to them. We started to drift through the undergrowth towards them, but we had only progressed a few yards when they took fright. They shuffled to and fro nervously for a minute or so, and then set off through the scrub, stalking along with the stately precision of slightly alarmed turkeys near Christmas-time, and very soon they disappeared. It seemed to me a terrible thought that—unless urgent measures are taken within the next ten years or so—this incredible bird might well become extinct. To a certain extent their mounds are preyed on by the introduced fox, who steals their eggs, but there is much more dangerous competition from rabbits and sheep who invade the Mallee and eat the seeds and plants that the bird lives on, and, by feeding both indiscriminately and voraciously, change the whole ecology of the Mallee scrub. When this happens the birds can no longer find food and so they have to move away (if there is anywhere to move to), or else die of starvation. Recently, too, there has been another threat to the bird in the shape of agriculture. At one time the Mallee scrub was inviolate, for the soil was considered too poor for crops, but now, with the discovery of a new chemical, it has been found that Mallee country can support crops of wheat. This means that vast areas of Mallee scrub which up until now have provided a sanctuary for the Mallee-Fowl, will be felled and planted and the birds will disappear. You cannot, of course, halt progress, but is it necessary to destroy everything in your path to achieve it? The Mallee-Fowl is one of the most incredible birds in the world, and for this reason alone deserves the right to exist. Much time and trouble has been taken to publicise and protect certain other members of the Australian fauna, and quite rightly; should it not be possible to do the same good promotion job for the Mallee-Fowl, and thus save it and some of its extraordinary environment for the enjoyment of future generations?

It wasn't far from Griffith that we came across a sight that illustrated very forcibly the necessity for conservation. Strung along a barbed wire fence that surrounded a huge field at the side of the road were twenty-eight Wedge-Tailed Eagles. They had been shot and then strung along the fence with their wings outspread as if crucified—a sort of avian Golgotha. Most of the birds were newly-fledged youngsters. As we were filming this macabre sight, a truck load of Australians passed.

'Don't waste your time on that,' they shouted, 'that's *nothing.*'

'What do they mean—that's nothing?' I asked Bevan. 'I would have thought that twenty-eight dead Wedge-Tails would have been considered a good bag by their standards.'

'No, they don't consider this a good bag,' said Bevan gloomily. 'You can sometimes see as many as fifty or more strung along a fence.'

Now, the Wedge-Tail is a large and powerful bird, and

undoubtedly does damage to the farmers by taking their lambs, so obviously, as a predator, it must be kept under control. Although at the moment the Wedge-Tail is fairly common, if this sort of slaughter increases, what chance of survival does the bird have? There are very few species prolific and cunning enough to combat this sort of depredation of their numbers. Considerably depressed by this gory sight, we continued on our way down to Melbourne where we were going to film, we hoped, a conservation success story starring what is, without doubt, Australia's most popular animal: the Koala bear.

Koala bears are, of course, not bears at all, but marsupials carrying their young in a pouch like the other Australian animals. At one time there was widespread shooting of the Koala bears for their skins. They made the most helpless of prey since they did not appear to have any fear of mankind and would simply sit in the trees staring down at the hunters while their companions were shot all around them. In 1924 over two million Koala skins were exported. This uncontrolled slaughter came at a time when the Koala bear colonies were being seriously depleted by a strange virus disease that was killing them off in hundreds, so that within a very short time the Koala was tottering on the borders of extinction. Fortunately, before it became too late, the Government stepped in and passed laws strictly protecting the Koalas, and slowly over the years their numbers have built up again. The problem with them now is that they tend to breed so successfully that they soon over-populate an area and start to eat out their food supply. It is at this juncture that the Wildlife Department has to step in and organise a bear hunt to catch up all the surplus Koalas and move them to a new feeding area, before they starve to death.

The scene of our bear hunt was some eucalyptus forest not far away from Melbourne, a place called by the unlikely name of Stoney Pines. It was a grey, windy, rainy day when we met up with the group of bear hunters who had arrived with a large truck containing the necessary accoutrements for the job, which included a large series of wooden crates in which to put the captured Koalas. Over the years the Wildlife Department has evolved an excellent method of capturing the bears without doing them any harm and without getting bitten themselves. The necessary equipment is a long, telescopic pole to the end of which is fixed a noose with a knot in it so that it cannot tighten round the Koala's neck and kill it. The other vital piece of equipment is a circular canvas sheet such as firemen use in rescuing people from burning buildings. The process is that you find your Koala, put a noose round its neck (which it readily agrees to), and you then pull it off the tree so that it falls into the canvas sheet, this being held out below by the rest of the bear hunters.

Having assembled the equipment, we set off through the trees and it was not very long before we came upon a group of eight Koala bears, three of them being mothers with babies. They just sat in the trees staring down at us vacantly and displaying no alarm whatsoever. I regret to say that my experience that day with Koala bears left me with an extremely low opinion of their mentality; like film starlets, they are delightful to look at but completely devoid of brain. The first one we caught was a big male, who allowed us to slip the noose over his head and continued to beam down at us, apparently completely unaware of what we were trying to do. When he felt the noose tighten, however, he clasped the tree more firmly with his curved claws and uttered a series of harsh growls that would have done justice to a tiger. Finally the tension on the rope became too great and he released his hold on the tree trunk and came crashing down into the canvas sheet; then we had the jolly job of getting the noose off his neck and putting him into one of the travelling crates. People who imagine that Koala bears are cuddly, inoffensive creatures should have a go at trying to get a noose off one. The Koala snarled and growled, slashed at us with his razor-sharp claws, and endeavoured to bite us whenever we got within range. Eventually, after a considerable amount of trouble, we bundled him, still growling ferociously, into the crate. It took us a couple of hours to catch up the little band of eight Koalas, and when we had them all safely boxed up, we drove off to the new area where they were to be released. It was curious that when we opened the cages and tipped the

Koalas out on to the ground, they stood there staring at us
and made absolutely no attempt to get away, and we had to
literally shoo them along the ground and up into the eucalyptus trees. They shinned up the smooth bark of the trees
effortlessly and settled among the branches, where they
suddenly burst into a chorus of wails and squeaky cries like
a group of distressed babies. One fascinating thing about the
Koala bears which I hoped we would be able to film, but
unfortunately we could not, was their method of weaning
their youngsters. When the baby Koala has left the pouch
and is ready to go on a solid diet, its mother, by some internal
alchemy, produces not excreta but a soft paste of semi-
digested eucalyptus leaves which resembles the tinned strained
foods which you give to babies, and this the baby Koala
feeds on until he is old enough to start eating the rather coarse

eucalyptus leaves off his own bat. This is, without doubt, the most amazing method any animal has of weaning its young.

Although the Koalas were enchanting to look at, I found them disappointing, completely lacking in personality, and having a rather vacuous approach to life in general. But how the skin hunters had the heart to shoot these trusting, attractive and harmless little animals in such quantity is a thing that defeats me. When we had successfully filmed the bear hunt and I had put a bandage on my thumb where a cuddly Koala (which I was endeavouring to help up a tree) had laid it open to the bone, we headed up-country towards Canberra. Here the CSIRO had a large research station in which they kept a great variety of marsupials and I was hoping that we would get some interesting film. What we actually saw and filmed there was one of the most remarkable things I have ever seen in my life, and it happened quite by chance.

CHAPTER 6

The Miracle Climb

In the next, that wild figure they saw
(As if stung by a spasm) plunge into a chasm.
Hunting of the Snark

THE FAUNA OF AUSTRALIA is something that makes any self-respecting naturalist excited. It has been described by one person as 'the attic of the world', the place where all the old things are stored; this is quite an apt description but is not strictly accurate. The two most interesting orders in Australia are the monotremes and the marsupials. The monotremes are the most primitive of mammals and have retained many of the characteristics which prove how mammals are descended from the reptiles. Superficially, the monotremes resemble conventional mammals in the sense that they breathe air, they are covered with fur, and they are warm blooded, but their chief and most astonishing reptilian characteristic is the fact that they lay eggs, and then, when the young hatch from the eggs, the parents feed them on milk. Most famous of the monotremes, of course, is the Duck-Billed Platypus, and another member of the group is the Echidna, that strange spiky creature that looks like a giant Martian hedgehog with long, pointed snout and heavy, outwardly curved claws on the front feet.

The marsupials are remarkable for a number of characteristics, best known of which is, of course, that the majority of them have a very short gestation period and give birth to their young in an almost embryonic condition. The baby then finds its way to the mother's pouch and continues its development there. The marsupials are very primitive creatures and it is lucky for them that the land bridge over which they spread into Australia was destroyed, for the more conventional mammals (such as tigers, leopards, lions and so on) would

have made short work of them. However, cut off as they were, with this great continent to themselves, they evolved along the most amazing lines—a sort of parallel evolution took place; instead of the great herds of hoofed animals that developed in Africa, Asia and America, you get the kangaroos and wallabies, who filled the same grazing niche. The places occupied by bushbabies or squirrels in other parts of the world were occupied in Australia by Possums and phalangers. A creature like the Badger has its equivalent in Australia in the Wombat, and the predators are represented by such things as the Tasmanian Wolf—not a true wolf, of course, but a marsupial, looking remarkably like its counterpart. So not only did the marsupials adapt themselves to the various niches but they came to resemble, in habits and sometimes in appearance, totally unrelated creatures that had evolved in other parts of the world: thus, the little Honey-Eaters look, at first glance, exactly like some of the smaller species of mouse; the Wombat resembles the Badger, the Tasmanian Wolf a member of the dog family, and there is even a Banded Anteater, to complete the picture. As an example of evolution the continent of Australia, with its monotremes and marsupials, is just as extraordinary as the Galapagos Islands, which so excited Darwin's imagination that he evolved the whole evolutionary thesis.

By and large, before the coming of man the marsupials had a pretty idyllic set-up. There were some predators in the shape of the Tasmanian Wolf, Wedge-Tailed Eagles, and the larger constricting snakes, but by and large they led a fairly trouble-free existence. Then came the aborigines and with them (one suspects) came the Dingo, a very cunning predator who rapidly became, together with his owners, the aborigines, Public Enemy Number One to the fauna. Although the Dingoes multiplied and spread, they did not appear to upset the balance of nature very much; neither did the aborigines, for there were too few of them, but with the advent of white men, the picture became very much blacker for the marsupials. Not only were their numbers depleted by human beings, but their habitat was invaded by introduced creatures such as the European fox and rabbit, the fox on the one hand acting as a predator and the rabbit acting as competition to the grazing marsupials for the food. Then came the sheep, and this is where the larger grazing marsupials started to acquire a bad reputation, for now they were in competition with the sheep and the sheep was more important to man. The farmers opened up whole new areas which, prior to this, had been arid and unsuitable country even for kangaroos and wallabies, and by driving wells and bore-holes they produced lush pastures for their sheep. They also found, to their annoyance, that the kangaroos and wallabies were deeply appreciative of this and poured into these new areas in numbers equalling, and in some cases exceeding, the sheep. So what is called the 'kangaroo menace' came into being.

Before you can control any wild animal, you have to know something about its basic biology; a simple policy of slaughter —quite apart from its threat to the survival of that particular species—is liable to do untold damage to the whole ecological structure of the country. An unbiological approach in different parts of the world to problems of this sort have, in the past, proved disastrous. So if an animal is becoming a pest you must set to work to learn everything you can about it; it is a case of 'knowing thine enemy'. The Wildlife Department of CSIRO was set up with just this object in mind. As soon as an animal is proclaimed a pest, CSIRO moves in and investigates the whole problem. They have to act, really, in the capacity of a High Court Judge, because in many cases a creature has been labelled a pest and, upon investigation, has proved to be considerably less of a pest than was thought. At Canberra, CSIRO has a large laboratory where one of their major studies at the moment is the two species of kangaroo—the Great Red and the Great Grey—so it was here that we went to get first-hand information on what would be the ultimate fate of the two largest and most spectacular marsupials in the world.

The team is headed by Harry Frith, who is one of Australia's foremost biologists and, among other things, famous for his brilliant ecological studies of various Australian ducks and geese and the Mallee-Fowl. He is a stocky, curly-haired man, his face browned and seamed by the sun and wind, the possessor of the most cynically amused pair of eyes

I have seen for a long time, and of a dry, caustic and deceptively laconic approach towards his work. He had already helped us by letter (and by briefly meeting Chris when he touched down on his way to New Zealand), and it was due to his advice that we had until then been so successful in our filming. Now we wanted to get some sequences on the work that was being done in Canberra, and for this we required Harry's permission and co-operation. I had never met him before and when we were ushered into his office I found him an intensely likeable but extremely intimidating sort of man. You felt that you had only to put a foot wrong to the slightest degree and he would clam up on you and become about as co-operative as Mount Everest. When I suggested that we would like to do some film sequences of their work, Harry stared at me moodily.

'I'll take you down to the yards,' he said, 'and introduce you to the boys. I don't mind you doing some film sequences but it's up to the boys. They're all working hard and it would mean they would have to waste a certain amount of time with you, so the decision must rest with them. If they tell you to push off, I can't do anything about it.' Then he smiled encouragingly at me.

Hoping that 'the boys' were going to be a trifle less misanthropic, we followed him down to the yards, which were a series of paddocks in which various species of kangaroo and wallaby were kept and bred. Here we were introduced to Geoff Sharman, a tall and utterly charming Australian scientist who is probably one of the world's foremost authorities on the biology of the marsupial. Having, as it were, pushed us into the lion's den, Harry then retreated to get on with his work, leaving me to try to make my mark with Geoff Sharman. This, to my relief, proved far easier than I had been led to anticipate; Geoff was not only a charming person, but so enthusiastic over his work that anybody who evinced the slightest interest in it became somebody worth talking to.

'We're looking for information that can be used for assessing the wild animals we find in the field. In other words, we're measuring the young in the pouch to see how they grow, and from this we can build up growth curves, which can be used to tell the age of the wild-caught young ones,' Geoff explained to me. 'We're also looking at their teeth. This is very important because the eruption pattern of the teeth seems to be a good way of telling the age of a kangaroo. This will give us some idea of the actual age structure of any population we are dealing with in the wilds. Once we've found that out here, the next thing is to go out and get a wild population of kangaroos marked in some way so that we can identify them. Then we examine their teeth every time we capture them, and see if we get the same kind of eruption pattern in the wild animal.'

'What's the breeding potentiality of a female kangaroo?' I asked him.

'Terrific,' Geoff said. 'It's like a Ford production belt. She can have one growing inside her, one in the pouch fastened to a teat and another one out of the pouch but still feeding from her.'

I asked him about the actual birth of the kangaroo, a thing that had always fascinated me, and it was at this juncture that he dropped his bomb-shell.

'Oh, the *birth*,' he said casually. 'I've got a bit of film I can show you of that.'

I stood rooted to the spot and stared at him.

'You've actually filmed it?' I said incredulously. 'But I thought that very few people had ever witnessed a birth, let alone got it on film.'

'Well, I think we're the first to get it on film,' he said. 'But we've got it down to quite a fine art here. We can tell you to within a few hours when the female is going to give birth.'

Chris and Jacquie were further down the yards, making love through the wire to an enchanting and precocious wallaby. I rushed down to Chris.

'Chris, do you know what Geoff Sharman's just told me?'

'What?' said Chris without interest, continuing his love-making with the wallaby.

'He's just told me that he's got some film of the actual birth of a kangaroo!'

'Oh?' said Chris, somewhat mystified by my obvious excitement, and appearing to be under the impression that to have a piece of film of a kangaroo birth was most common-place. 'So what?'

'What do you mean, so what?' I said. 'You moron, don't you realise that very few people have ever *seen* a kangaroo birth, and I didn't think anyone had ever *filmed* it. In fact, I think that Geoff is probably the first person to do so.'

'Um,' said Chris, brightening a little, 'is it very interesting?'

'Well, of course it's interesting,' I said. 'The thing's only about the size of a hazelnut when it's born—it's virtually an embryo, in fact, and once it's born it then has to climb all the way up its mother and get into the pouch.'

'That sounds as though it would make a good sequence,' said Chris, displaying more enthusiasm. 'I wonder if Geoff would let us use his film?'

We went over to where Geoff had extracted a hairless and rather revolting-looking baby kangaroo from its mother's pouch and was solemnly weighing it in a cloth bag.

'Geoff,' I said wheedlingly, 'is there any chance of you letting us have that piece of film on the kangaroo birth?'

'Sure,' he said instantly, and then dampened my hopes by adding, 'but you'll have to check with Harry first.'

'Oh yes,' I said, 'I'll do that, but look, if the film for some reason is not suitable, is there a chance of our re-shooting it?'

'Oh yes,' said Geoff, 'that's easy enough, we've got several females that will be ready fairly soon, but again I can't let you do that without permission from Harry.'

'But,' I said, getting things quite clear, 'you'd have no objection to our doing it providing Harry says it's okay?'

'None at all,' said Geoff. 'I'd be glad to help.'

We had arranged to meet Harry for lunch and during it I cunningly kept off the subject of marsupial births until Harry had engulfed several lamb chops and a couple of pints of beer and was beginning to look a little bit benign round the edges. Then I took a deep breath, and started.

'Harry, Geoff Sharman tells me that you have some film of a kangaroo birth,' I said.

Harry eyed me inimically.

'Yes,' he said cautiously.

'I suppose it wouldn't be possible for us to have a print of that to include in the series?' I said.

'I don't see why not,' said Harry, 'but I'm afraid the decision must rest with Geoff.'

'Oh,' I said, 'well that's all right then, he has already said yes, but he had to have your confirmation.'

Harry ruminated on this and there was a faint twinkle in his eye.

'But supposing,' I said, hastily pouring him out another glass of beer, 'that the film is not entirely suitable for television?'

'Well,' said Harry, 'let's suppose it, what then?'

'Well, would it be possible to re-shoot it?'

'I presume,' said Harry dryly, 'that you've already got Geoff Sharman's permission for this?'

'Well, in a tentative sort of way,' I admitted, 'but he said that you'd have to give the final word.'

'I don't mind,' said Harry. 'If Geoff feels he can fit it in with his work and if he can organise it for you, I don't mind a bit.'

I heaved a deep sigh of relief and beamed at Christopher.

'This, dear boy,' I said, 'is going to be the climax of the series. If we get it!'

After lunch we went jubilantly back to Geoff Sharman to tell him that Harry had agreed. Geoff was delighted and had very soon fixed up a projector in his room in order to show us the coveted piece of film. This, however, proved disappointing, for although it showed the details that were of importance from Geoff's point of view as a scientist, it was unsuitable for television. This meant that we would have to put into operation Plan Two, which was to re-film the whole thing.

'I think Pamela is probably our best bet,' said Geoff, staring at a doe-eyed Grey Kangaroo who was busy picking up pieces of carrot in her monkey-like front paws and chewing them vigorously. 'She is due in about a week's time and, anyway, if we fail with her we can fall back on Marilyn or Marlene, who should be giving birth shortly afterwards.'

'What's the drill then?' I asked.

'Well, the first signs,' said Geoff, 'are that she starts to clean out the pouch. This generally happens a few hours before the birth itself. If you are somewhere within easy reach, we can 'phone you and it will give you time to set up the lights and the cameras.'

'Won't the cameras and lights worry her?' asked Chris.

'I shouldn't think so for a moment,' said Geoff, 'she's a very placid creature.'

So began a period of waiting, while we hovered round Pamela like expectant fathers, filming her every move. But we wanted to try to show the full picture of the kangaroo problem as well as the birth, if we were lucky enough to get it, and so Harry, together with Bevan Bowan, took us out to a 'spread' not far from Canberra (a tiny little smallholding of some 200,000 acres) on which they were investigating another facet of the kangaroo's biology.

'We're endeavouring to find out a number of different things,' said Harry as we bumped our way over the sun-bleached grass in among the eucalyptus trees. 'Firstly, we want to know how the groups of kangaroos move—how much territory they cover in, say, a week or a month. This we can only do by catching them up and marking them, so that they are recognisable from a distance, through field-glasses. We do this by putting a coloured collar on them, with a number. You'll see how we do it presently. The other thing we are trying to find out is whether or not the kangaroo is a selective feeder. Now take East Africa; there's a country that supports vast quantities of game animals and the reason they haven't turned it into a gigantic dust bowl is because they are selective feeders, so that one species of ante-lope feeds on a certain series of plants and ignores others, which are, in turn, eaten by a different species of antelope. Where your undermining of the country and the creation of erosion comes in, is when you introduce a species that is an indiscriminate feeder. In East Africa the damage is largely done by the huge herds of skinny and totally unattractive cattle, and flocks of goats which just chew up everything in sight. It's possible that we might find a roughly similar situation here. It's possible that we might find that the kangaroo is a selective feeder and therefore, in fact, does less damage to the country than the rabbit or the sheep, although, of course, if this proves to be so, we are going to have the devil's own job persuading the sheep farmer that this is the case.'

He chuckled reminiscently.

'I remember up north,' he said, 'when I went about telling the rice farmers that the Magpie Goose was not the pest that they claimed, I nearly got lynched on several occasions, and once I was pulled out of my car by a giant of a man, who would have flattened me if it had not been for the fact that I luckily had Bevan with me.'

'I never knew conservation could be so bloodthirsty,' I said.

'You'd be surprised,' said Harry. 'No, but it's quite obvious that the kangaroo is a problem. I've known of farms where the kangaroo population has outnumbered the sheep population by about three to one. Obviously this is detrimental to the sheep farmers' interests and something must be done about it. What we hope to achieve is a control over the kangaroo so that we don't have to exterminate them. I see no reason why, if we can learn to control them successfully, we should not have both kangaroos and sheep.'

We had been driving for some considerable time along the edge of a barbed wire fence and we came now to a curious structure at one corner of this gigantic field. A sort of funnel had been built alongside the fence, using the fence as one wall and wire netting for the other. This funnel led into a small paddock some thirty feet square.

'This,' said Harry, 'is the trap. Now the art of catching the kangaroos is this; first you find your kangaroos and then you chivvy them gently until they're heading along the fence. Gradually you increase speed, but you have to do it very cautiously—if you are too quick, you'll panic them and they'll jump over the fence and get away. You must chivvy them at just the right speed to keep them on the go so they'll hop right down that fence, through the funnel and into that trap, and then you've got to run like hell to catch them before they jump out of the trap.'

He leant out of the window to shout some instructions to Bevan, who was driving the other Land-Rover, and then both vehicles were off, circling the paddock, searching for the kangaroos. Travelling at 35 miles an hour over that bumpy terrain, swerving in and out of the eucalyptus trees, was quite a hair-raising experience. The first creatures we disturbed were a flock of Emus, who behaved in a fairly typically stupid manner. Instead of breaking away from us, they seemed so panic-stricken and fascinated that they ran to try to cut across our bows. Having got just in front of us, they then appeared to become quite hysterical and incapable of running to one side, and thumped along in front of us, their great feet almost touching their chins in their efforts to out-run us. Presently we came to a fence and, to my astonishment, the Emus made no effort to stop, but just ran straight at it. One went through, leaving a cloud of feathers behind him, but the other one struck the barbed wire at an angle and bounced off. He staggered back and then took another run at it, and this time he was successful, although he, too, left enough feathers behind him to stuff a small cushion.

'That's why the farmers don't like Emus, either,' said Harry, 'they do the hell of a lot of damage to the fences.'

We progressed for about another quarter of an hour, then suddenly heard Bevan honking his horn. Looking over, we saw a flock of about ten Grey Kangaroos sitting stock-still at the edge of a little wood, staring at us with their ears pricked. Harry swerved violently round a tree to correct our course and we headed straight for the kangaroos, while Bevan

drove out further to prevent them from breaking back. As we drew close to them they started hopping off in a rather nonchalant fashion, but as the vehicles accelerated the kangaroos panicked and started running away in real earnest. It was fascinating to watch them taking those prodigious leaps, using their tails purely as a balancing organ. Soon we had chivvied them round so that they were lolloping along the length of the fence towards the trap, and here both vehicles suddenly put on a burst of speed. I would not have thought it was possible to drive through that sort of country at 50 miles an hour, but we did it. Not only did you have to cling to your seat to prevent being thrown out through the top of the roof or through the windscreen, but you also had to be

prepared for the violent swerves that had to be made to circumnavigate the many small trees that dotted the grassland.
The kangaroos were by now thoroughly panic-stricken, and
although some of them stopped and made an attempt to leap
the fence, we always managed to prevent them by putting
on another burst of speed. At last, the trap came into sight.
A final burst of speed from the two Land-Rovers and the
panic-stricken kangaroos raced down the funnel and found
themselves at a dead end. We clamped on our brakes, leapt
out of the Land-Rover and raced down the fence into the trap
amongst the milling mob of kangaroos. There is only one
way to catch a kangaroo successfully and that is to avoid, at
all costs, his massive and potentially lethal hind legs, and
grasp him firmly by the tail. He then proceeds to bounce in
front of you until he is exhausted or until someone else comes
to your rescue and grabs other parts of his anatomy. This
we proceeded to do until we had all the kangaroos firmly
hogtied. Under the baking sun, the poor things were panting
and sweating with the exertion and the heat. Carefully each
one was dressed up in a neat, celluloid collar in different colours
and with a different number on each, and we then took them,
one by one, outside the trap and let them go. Most of them
hopped away rapidly and with obvious relief, but there was
one small one who, when placed on the ground, remained
standing stock-still, staring into space. Harry went up behind
it and patted it gently on the rump, whereupon the kangaroo
turned on him ferociously, and an extremely amusing boxing
match took place, with Harry endeavouring to shoo the
kangaroo away and the kangaroo endeavouring to get its
own back on Harry. As the kangaroo only measured about
three feet high and Harry was a good six feet, the marsupial's
attacks on him had all the temerity of David's encounter with
Goliath. At last, however, it decided that its desire to disem-

bowel Harry was doomed to failure and so, with a certain amount of reluctance, it hopped off to join the others.

It was now getting near the time when we could expect the birth and so we took up residence in a motel, conveniently situated about half a mile down the road from the laboratories. This was when Pamela decided that she was going to give us a run for our money. For three days she designed a series of false alarms for us, and she timed these so cleverly that they did the maximum amount of damage to our nervous systems. Suddenly, as we were in the middle of lunch, or in the bath, or just drifting cosily off to sleep, there would be a frantic telephone message from Geoff to say that he thought, from Pamela's behaviour, that the birth was imminent. If we happened to be bathing or sleeping it meant a frantic scramble into our clothes, a wild gallop out into the courtyard with our equipment, and we would pile into the Land-Rover and drive off with a deafening roar. Our rather curious actions seemed to mystify the owner of the motel, as well as the other guests, and they started giving us such peculiar looks that, in self-defence, we had to explain what we were trying to achieve, whereupon they all took an intense interest in the whole matter and would rush to the windows to cheer us on our way as we galloped towards the Land-Rover, dropping bits of equipment and tripping each other up in our haste. Every time we got down to the yards, however, Pamela would be munching some delicacy and would look up with a faintly surprised air that we should have bothered to pay her yet another visit.

Then came the evening when, in the middle of dinner, the motel proprietor came galloping into the dining-room and informed us that Geoff Sharman had just 'phoned and said that *quite definitely* Pamela was going to give birth at any minute. Knocking over a bottle of wine and leaving our napkins

strewn across the floor like autumn leaves, we fled from the
dining-room, pursued by cheers and shouts of 'Good luck'
from our fellow guests. Chris, in his eagerness, started the
Land-Rover so quickly that I was left with one foot inside and
one on the ground when he was changing into top; with a
fearful effort that almost dislocated my spine, I managed to
scramble in, and we zoomed down the road to the laboratories.

'She's definitely going to do it this time,' said Geoff. 'I'm
quite certain of it.'

She could not have picked a better time. It was pitch dark,
bitterly cold, and everything was drenched in dew. Hastily
we rigged up the arc lights and got the cameras in position.
Pamela was sitting, leaning against a fence and getting on with
the good work of cleaning out her pouch. This she did very
fastidiously, using her front paws. The pouch, when un-
tenanted, tends to exude a waxy substance similar to the wax
in a human ear, and it was this that she was cleaning out, carefully combing the furry interior of the pouch with her claws.
We filmed her doing this and then sat and gazed at her
expectantly. She continued cleaning her pouch out for about
half an hour, stared round moodily, then hopped down to the
far end of the paddock and started to eat.

'I think we've got a little time to wait,' said Geoff.

'Are you quite sure that this isn't another of her false
alarms?' I asked.

'Oh no,' said Geoff, 'this is the real thing; she wouldn't
clean out her pouch as thoroughly as that if she wasn't going
to give birth.'

We sat in the freezing cold and stared at Pamela and she
stared back at us, her jaws moving rhythmically.

'Let's go into the hut while we're waiting,' said Geoff, 'it will be a little bit warmer. If your hands get too cold, you won't be able to manipulate your equipment.'

We crowded into the tiny shed, where I produced, to the delight of the assembled company, a bottle of whisky that I had had the foresight to bring with me. We took it in turns, between drinks, to go out and peer hopefully in Pamela's direction, but nothing happened.

'Jolly experience, this,' said Jim, 'sitting up all night, sloshing whisky and waiting for a kangaroo to be born. Never had an experience like it.'

'Well, you'll be able to add it to your repertoire of unusual events that have taken place in your life,' said Chris, 'together with the hair drier and being sick on a pontoon bridge.'

'What,' enquired Geoff, 'is all this about hair driers and pontoon bridges?'

We explained that Jim was not a normal mortal and went through life involving himself in the most unlikely situations.

'You should get him to tell you about the time he got a bicycle jammed in the chimney,' I said.

'What?' said Geoff. 'How on earth did he manage that?'

'He's lying,' said Jim excitedly. 'I never did anything of the sort.'

'I definitely remember you telling me,' I said. 'I can't recall the exact details but I remember it was a fascinating story.'

'But how,' said Geoff, his scientific interest deeply aroused, 'did you get a bicycle jammed up a chimney?'

'He's lying, I tell you,' said Jim. 'I've never owned a bicycle, let alone got it jammed in a chimney.'

By now Geoff and all his co-workers were quite convinced that Jim *had* got a bicycle jammed in a chimney and was merely being modest about this achievement, and they spent the next hour endeavouring to work out how he could have managed this feat, with Jim getting more and more irritable with each passing suggestion.

It came as somewhat of a relief to him when one of Geoff's assistants appeared in the doorway of the hut and said, 'Action stations, I think we're off.'

We scrambled out of the hut and took up our positions. Pamela was moving about, looking rather uncomfortable. Presently, against the fence of the paddock, she dug a shallow hole in the ground and then took up a position in it, with her tail sticking out between her hind legs and her back resting against the fence. She sat like this for a few minutes and then obviously started feeling uncomfortable again, for she lay down on her side for a few seconds and then stood up and moved around for a bit. Then she went back to the hole she had dug and again sat with her tail sticking out between her legs and her back against the fence. She was completely unperturbed by the fact that arc lights, two cine cameras and the eyes of about a dozen people were fixed on her.

'You'd better start the cameras now,' said Geoff.

The cameras started to whirr and, as if on cue, the baby was born. It dropped out on to Pamela's tail and lay there, a pinky-white, glistening blob no longer than the first joint of my little finger.

Although I knew roughly what to expect, the whole performance was one of the most miraculous and incredible things that I have ever seen in all the years that I have been watching animals. The baby was, to all intents and purposes, an embryo —it had, in fact, been born after a gestation period of only 33 days; it was blind and its hind legs, neatly crossed over each other, were powerless; yet in this condition it had been expelled into the world. As if this was not enough of a handicap, it now had to climb up through the fur on Pamela's stomach until it found the entrance to the pouch. This was

really the equivalent of a blind man, with both legs broken, crawling through thick forest to the top of Mount Everest, for the baby got absolutely no assistance from Pamela at all. We noticed (and we have it on film to prove it) that the mother does *not* help the baby by licking a path through the fur, as is so commonly reported. The baby, as soon as it was born, with a curious, almost fish-like wiggle, left the mother's tail and started to struggle up through the fur. Pamela ignored it.

She bent over and licked her nether regions and her tail clean and then proceeded to clean her fur *behind* the baby as it was climbing, for it was obviously leaving a trail of moisture through her hair. Occasionally her tongue passed over the baby, but I am certain that this was more by accident than design. Slowly and valiantly the pulsating little pink blob struggled on through the thick fur. From the moment it was born to the moment it found the rim of the pouch took some ten minutes. That a creature weighing only a gramme (the weight of five or six pins) could have achieved this climb was a miracle in itself, but, having got to the rim of the pouch, it had another task ahead of it. The pouch is approximately the size of a large, woman's handbag. Into this the Lilliputian kangaroo had to crawl and then search the vast, furry area in order to find the teat; this search might take him anything up to twenty minutes. Having found the teat, he would then fasten on to it, whereupon it would swell in his mouth, thus making him adhere to it firmly—so firmly, indeed, that if you try to pull a baby kangaroo off its mother's teat, you will tear the soft mouth parts and cause bleeding. This has given rise to the entirely erroneous idea that baby kangaroos are born on the teat, i.e. develop from the teat itself, like a sort of bud.

Finally the baby hauled itself over the edge of the rim of the pouch and disappeared into the interior, and we could switch off the cameras and the lights. We had got some remarkable and unique film and both Chris and Jim were ecstatic. For me it had been an unforgettable experience, and I am sure that even the most hardened anti-kangaroo sheep farmer would have been impressed by the baby's grim determination to perform its herculean task. After being cast out into the world only half formed, and being made to undertake this prodigious climb, I felt that the baby kangaroo thoroughly deserved his life in his fur-lined, centrally-heated pram with its built-in milk bar. I hoped, very sincerely, that the work that was being done by Harry Frith, Geoff Sharman and the other members of the team would find a way to preserve the largest of the marsupials from complete eradication.

THE
VANISHING JUNGLE

The Beaver's best course was, no doubt, to procure
A second-hand dagger-proof coat—

Hunting of the Snark

THE ARRIVAL

I WAS SITTING under a tree covered with huge scarlet flowers, and meditatively sipping a beer, when I heard the boat. I was seated high on an escarpment overlooking several thousand miles of forest—a Persian carpet of greens, reds, golds and russets—and below me the Tembeling river wound its way between steep banks, brown and glinting as a slow-worm. I was, in fact, sitting outside the rest house on the edge of Malaya's biggest National Park, an enormous block of forest that stretched away in every direction.

I took another sip of beer and listened to the stutter of the outboard engine growing louder and louder. I wondered who the new arrivals were. Presently the boat hove into view and headed for the landing stage below me. As far as I could see it was crammed to the gills with an extremely convivial party of Sikhs who, to relieve the tedium of the journey up-river, had partaken heartily—if unwisely—of some form of intoxicating liquid. I watched with interest as they landed uncertainly and wended their way, laughing and joking, up the hill. They passed me sitting in solitary state under my tree, and waved extravagant greetings and bowed. I bowed and waved back, and they made their way towards another small rest house which stood a few hundred yards off among the trees. The last of their party, who had stayed behind to give some rather incoherent instructions to the boatman, now came panting up the hill. He was a fine-looking man of about sixty with a magnificent Father Christmas beard, and with his turban slightly askew.

'Good evening, good evening,' he called when he was within earshot, waving and beaming at me, 'my God what a vunderful day, eh?'

I had spent a hot, sticky and profitless day in extremely prickly undergrowth, being sucked dry by leeches, but I didn't want to dampen my new friend's enthusiasm.

'Wonderful!' I shouted back.

He came panting up to me and stood there, grinning.

'Ve have come on a fishing expedition, you know,' he explained.

'Really?' I said. 'Is there good fishing here?'

'Vunderful, *vunderful*,' he said, 'best fishing in Malaya.'

He eyed my glass of beer with the air of one who had never seen such a phenomenon before, but was willing to try anything once.

'Will you have a drink?' I asked.

'My dear sir, you are too kind,' he said, seating himself with alacrity.

I called the steward, who brought a large tankard of beer which my new friend seized firmly, in case it tried to escape.

'Your very good health,' he said, and drank half of it at one gulp without pausing for breath.

He belched thoughtfully and wiped the froth off his moustache with a spotless handkerchief.

'I need that,' he explained untruthfully, 'hot vork travelling.'

For the next half-hour he regaled me with a complicated and extremely amusing lecture on the art of fishing, and I was quite sorry when eventually he rose unsteadily to his feet and said that he must go.

'You must let us return your hospitality,' he said earnestly.

'Come over to our little house at about six and have a tiny drink, eh?'

I had had experience of tiny drinks with Sikhs before, and the tiny drink generally extended into the small hours of the morning, but he was so eager that it would have been churlish to refuse. So I accepted, and he meandered away, waving cheerfully to me over his shoulder. Presently Jacquie and Chris joined me.

'Who,' enquired Chris, 'was your friend—Santa Claus?'

'He's a very amusing Sikh,' I said, 'and he's invited me over for a drink at six.'

'I hope you didn't accept,' said Jacquie in alarm, 'you know what these drinking orgies are like.'

'Yes I have,' I said, 'I couldn't very well refuse. But have no fear, I shall get Chris to come and rescue me at seven.'

'Why *me*?' enquired Chris bitterly. 'I'm supposed to be a producer, not a sort of travelling Alcoholics Anonymous.'

At six o'clock, bathed and changed, I presented myself at the small rest house and was welcomed in by the fishing party. It consisted of five individuals, four of whom were tall, well-built men, while the fifth was a tiny and earnest-looking little man wearing an enormous pair of horn-rimmed spectacles. After the introductions had been made and they had poured me out a drink of such massive proportions that I mentally praised my foresight in getting Chris to rescue me, we started the usual conversation about fishing and animal photography. When we had exhausted these subjects there was a slight pause, while we all had another drink. Then suddenly (and to this day I cannot remember how) we were discussing homosexuality. This was a fine, rich subject for discussion and we explored it thoroughly, ranging from Oscar Wilde to Petronius via the Shakespeare Sonnets and Burton's *Arabian Nights*, taking in the *Kama Sutra* and *The Perfumed Garden* en route. At this point Chris arrived, and was thrust into a chair and given a drink, without causing the slightest ripple on the surface of our train of thought. During all this the earnest little man with the outsize spectacles had sat there, clasping his glass and surveying each speaker through his spectacles, but contributing nothing to the conversation. Eventually (when we had dealt at length with the decline and fall of the Roman Empire), we felt we had exhausted the subject and we all fell silent. It was the earnest little man's great moment. He leant forward and peered at me and cleared his throat. We all looked at him expectantly.

'What *I* say, Mr. Durrell,' he said impressively, summing up our flights of rhetoric in one pungent phrase, 'what *I* say, is that every man should have his hobby.'

CHAPTER 7

The Singers in the Trees

While strange creepy creatures came out of their dens,
And watched them with wondering eyes.

Hunting of the Snark

THE TAMAN NEGARA—which used to be called The King George V National Park—was created in 1937. It is a gigantic slab of untouched forest measuring some 1,677 square miles, spreading into the States of Kelantan, Pahang and Trengganu. Only a small portion of the Park is easily accessible to the average visitor; the rest of it can be investigated, but only with extreme difficulty. Therefore, there are some areas of the Park which are still unexplored. Within its boundaries you can see, if you are lucky, nearly every member of the Malayan jungle fauna. Probably one of the Park's most important functions is that it provides a sanctuary for the few remaining specimens of the Sumatran Rhino. There are probably not more than a few hundred of these creatures left in existence. Like all the other Asiatic rhinos, they have been unmercifully hunted in order to procure their horns, which are ground into powder and shipped to China, where it is sold at exorbitant sums to aged, decrepit or sterile Chinese who have the touching belief that it will act as an aphrodisiac. Why a country so hideously over-populated should waste its time and energy in such a pursuit defeats the imagination, but because of this belief nearly all the Asian species of rhino have been reduced in numbers to the very borders of extermination and, because they are getting increasingly hard to find, a similar attack is now being made on the rhinos of Africa.

The fact that the Park was full of wildlife meant nothing. In that dense and extremely tall forest, the difficulty was firstly to come into contact with the animals, and secondly, once you had made contact with them, to try to film them. But gradually, little by little, we managed to build up a picture of the inhabitants of the Park and their daily routine. There were the small herds of Seladang, for example, a powerful, handsome species of wild ox with their dark chocolate brown or black coats and white socks and handsomely curved, thick white horns. They would graze in small clearings in the forest throughout the morning until the sun became increasingly hot, when they would retreat into the cooler recesses among the trees, where they would muse and doze until the cool of the evening; then they would rouse themselves and spend the night drifting through the forest in search of food. The Seladang is so big and powerful and so quickly aroused to terrible defensive rage that it has few enemies brave enough to tackle it. The two chief predators are, of course, the tiger and the leopard. The tiger appears to be on the decline in Malaya, but the leopard is still relatively common. While the tiger will tackle, on occasions, a fully grown Seladang, the leopard, being a smaller and less powerful cat, generally prefers to try its hand at the youngsters; but there is easier game in the forest than Seladang.

For the great majority of the forest creatures, night is the time when they are up and about. The sun sets and there is a very brief twilight when the whole forest and the sky are washed in a pale, apple-green light.

Suddenly the whole sky becomes freckled with tiny black dots that drift over the tree tops in great waves like columns of smoke. They are the large, honking, leathery-winged Fruit Bats on their way into the interior of the Park to search for food. All day long they have hung upside down in a dead tree some two miles down-stream. Why they chose this leafless tree I could never make out, but they hung there in great clusters like badly made umbrellas, occasionally stretching their wings out and fanning themselves vigorously to try to cool their bodies under the torrid rays of the sun. Once the bats were aloft in the sky, honking and flapping their way in untidy clouds towards their feeding grounds, it was the signal that the night shift had taken over.

Now the Seladang started to move, the tigers and the leopards yawned and stretched and sniffed appreciatively, gourmet fashion, at the exciting night-time smells of the forest. Now the tiny, mahogany-coloured Mouse Deer appeared, neatly camouflaged with white spots and stripes, their fragile legs no thicker than a pencil. Knowing that they were favourite food for nearly every predator, they lived in a permanent state of high tension bordering on hysteria, and seemed to shimmer through the leaves and low undergrowth. The slightest sound or movement and they would flash away with such rapidity that the eye could not follow them and you wondered how on earth any predator was skilful enough to catch them. Up in the canopy of the forest, where the day-time chorus of those insane and incessant zitherers, the cicadas, had now given place to a more fully fledged orchestra of tree frogs, various other creatures would be uncurling themselves and thinking about food. The Tree Shrews—squirrel-like but with long, pointed faces and little pink noses that were perpetually twitching like geiger counters—would scuttle along the branches and pass from tree to tree along the lianas.

These lashed the trees together and acted like some curious vegetable switch-back through the forest. At first glance, you might be pardoned for thinking that a Tree Shrew was a rather unsuccessful cross between a squirrel and a rat, and you would be amazed and possibly indignant if somebody suggested that you were looking at a relative of yours, but the Tree Shrew is related to the great group of primates which includes everything from Bush Babies to Apes, from Aborigines to Members of Parliament. It is, in fact, from such a

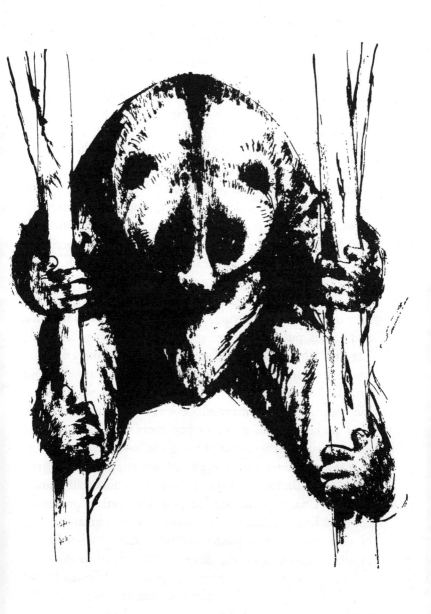

lowly creature as the Tree Shrew that the whole primate group has evolved, but when you see them fussing around the tree tops, chittering shrilly at each other, or scrunching up beetles with all the aplomb of a debutante engulfing ortolans, there appears to be no shadow on its conscience.

Another night-time prowler was the Slow Loris, which looks somewhat like a miniature, silvery-pink teddy bear. Its enormous, owl-like eyes stare wildly through the branches as though the creature were on the borders of an acute and sustained nervous breakdown. This effect is enhanced by the fact that it has a dark rim of fur round each eye which makes it look as though it is suffering from two permanent black eyes. Normally the Loris moves with all the speed and bounce of an elderly and excessively corpulent clergyman suffering from angina pectoris and in-growing toe-nails. This slow movement is, of course, useful to him in capturing his prey, but it is deceiving, for try to catch a Loris up a tree and he will put on a turn of speed that is amazing. After the Loris the Binturongs would appear, strange creatures that look like badly made hearthrugs, with tufted ears and rather curious, oriental looking eyes. They would plod their way through the branches in a somnambulistic sort of way, making use of their prehensile tails as an anchor every time they stopped. Anything is grist to the Binturong's mill—fruit, unripe nuts, tree frogs, baby birds or eggs—all are engulfed with great relish. The Binturong is another of those unfortunate animals that the Chinese have decided possesses magical properties, and so its blood, bones and internal organs are in great demand; in consequence, this placid, harmless and completely un-magical creature is on the decrease throughout its range.

Once the whole forest is up and about, then the last but by no means the least of the animals makes its appearance: the elephant. Throughout the hot day they have been musing

and swaying in some cool recess of the forest, but now they
rouse themselves and drift to their feeding grounds like great
grey shadows, their bodies moving through the undergrowth
so gently that the only sound you can hear is the faintest
whisper of leaves, as though caused by a tiny breeze. Sometimes, in fact, a herd of elephants will move so cautiously and
silently through the tangled undergrowth that you are only
aware of their presence by the one noise over which they have
no control—the loud, prolonged and sonorous rumbling of
their tummies. Elephants adore water, and even the elderly
and more sedate matriarchs and patriarchs of herds will get
positively skittish when there is any water around.

We watched and filmed an old female with her baby
which, towards evening, she had brought down to a stream
in order to cool off. She stepped into the shallow water and
paused, musing to herself, as if to test the temperature of the
water; then she waded out and slowly lowered herself until

she was lying down. The baby, who had had a certain difficulty in negotiating the steep bank of the stream, arrived at the water's edge and gave a ridiculous squeak of delight, like the noise of a small, falsetto tin bugle. He then hurled himself into the stream and rushed across to where his mother was lying, placidly squirting water over her head and back. To the female, of course, the water was not deep, but the baby was well out of his depth; this, however, did not deter him in the slightest. He just disappeared beneath the surface of the water and used his trunk like a periscope. Having reached his mother's side, he scrambled out on to her wet flank, giving little squeals of pleasure to himself. He then evolved a game which I could only presume to be the elephant equivalent of playing submarines. Disappearing beneath the water, he circled round and round his mother, attacking her from different angles under the surface until she reached down into the water with her trunk and hauled him

up by his ear. We watched them for an hour or so, until it grew too dark to see, and the baby was still indulging in his underwater game with undiminished vigour.

By the time dawn comes to the forest, in a blaze of scarlet, gold and blue stripes, most of the nocturnal animals have retreated to holes in trees or caves, and now the diurnal animals take over. There is a great, echoing burst of bird

song, and in the morning dew the cicadas start zithering experimentally, getting in trim for the great orchestral effort that they will produce during the heat of the day. Then the forest suddenly rings with its most characteristic noise— the wild, exuberant cries of the gibbons. These singers in the trees are found everywhere, and at all times of the day you can hear their joyous, whooping cries that rise to a crescendo and then trail away into a hysterical giggle. The biggest of the gibbon family is the Siamang, a huge black ape whose throat, when he sings, swells up to the size of a small grape-fruit and produces the most astonishingly resonant volume of sound.

The only day we were lucky enough to see Siamang turned out to be quite an auspicious day from a number of points of view. It had started early in the morning with Chris insisting that he wanted to get some shots of Jacquie and myself on top of a hill that lay downstream. No amount of argument on anyone's part would convince him that these shots could equally well be done in a more accessible position, and so we headed downstream in a large canoe fitted with an outboard engine. We landed on a long white shingle beach and then, humping our heavy equipment, we entered the forest and started to climb. The hill got steeper and steeper and we got hotter and hotter. The low undergrowth in the Malayan forest has evolved some of the spikiest and most malignant bushes it has ever been my misfortune to come into contact with. Delicate, pale green, fern-like growths shimmer at you innocently. They look so fragile that you feel a harsh word would make them wilt and die, and so you brush them out of your path with great tenderness, only to find that the underside of each of these innocent looking fronds is furnished with a set of curved, needle-sharp hooks. Immediately, the plant sinks these vegetable grappling-irons into your flesh and clothing, and the more you struggle the more deeply involved you become, until you begin to feel like—and are bleeding as copiously as—an early Christian martyr. Jim had an even greater penchant for getting himself caught by these evil plants than I had, and so our progress up the hillside was slow. We had to keep stopping and disentangling him, at the same time trying to stifle his screams for fear that they would frighten away any animals which we might otherwise be lucky enough to see. Eventually, bloodstained and sweaty, we arrived at a small clearing at the top of the hill and sat down to have a rest.

Now, most of the Malayan forest is infested with leeches, but for some reason or other this particular clearing had more than its fair share, and they seemed to be twice as voracious. When we sat down in the clearing there was not a leech to be seen. Whether they get to know of your presence by vibrations of the ground as you move, or whether they smell you, is a thing that I could never satisfactorily decide, but no sooner had we sat down and lit cigarettes than out of the undergrowth on all sides of the clearing there appeared a creeping carpet of them, humping their way across the leaves like small black looper caterpillars. Occasionally they would stand right up on end, waving their heads about as if they were testing the air for scent. It was utterly impossible, wherever you went in the forest, to keep the leeches off you; all you could do was hope that they would not attach themselves to some inaccessible nook or cranny of your anatomy. They will creep through the tiniest places and their movements are so gossamer light that you do not know they are on you until you suddenly see their black bodies, bloated with blood, hanging from you like small figs. The only two methods of dealing with them, always provided you know they are on you, is a lighted cigarette end or a pinch of common salt.

Both these methods of attack make the leeches release their hold and drop off. Should you be unwise enough to pull them off, they leave their mouthparts embedded in your flesh and you get a nice suppurating sore for your pains. So we sat there, trying to recover our breath, while the swarms of leeches engulfed us.

'Charming!' said Jim bitterly. 'I did manage to save half an ounce of blood from those damned plants and now even that's going to be drained out of me by these filthy things.'

His temper was not improved when Chris, in a rather crestfallen manner, admitted that the top of the hill was not suitable for the shots that he had in mind after all. So, carrying a full cargo of leeches, we picked up the equipment and staggered down the hill again. When we arrived on the sandbank, we all discreetly stripped and de-leeched each other with the aid of cigarettes.

'Now,' said Jim, pulling on his trousers, 'what jolly little thing would Chris like us to do now? How about swimming across the river, Gerry? With a bit of luck you might see a crocodile. What a good sequence that would make!'

'Actually, what I was thinking,' said Chris musingly, 'is that if you took the canoe up those rapids there, we could get some rather impressive shots.'

I gazed at the area he indicated, where some great brown slabs of rock bisected the river like a row of ancient and discoloured dentures. Between these rocks the water was squeezed and tangled and gushed in a series of rapids with all the force of a fire hose.

'Are you nuts?' I enquired of our producer.

'No,' said Chris, 'it looks much worse than it is, actually.'

'Yes!' said Jim enthusiastically. 'And think of the thrill after you've done it of being told he doesn't want the shots after all.'

After a certain amount of argument we decided to leave the casting vote to the boatman. He, to my intense annoyance, said that he would be only too charmed to take the canoe up the rapids, so there was nothing for it. Jim and Chris took up their stations by the camera, while Jacquie and I climbed into the canoe and set off. The canoe had seemed fairly precarious when we had started off in her that morning, but she seemed to become frailer and frailer and less and less seaworthy the nearer we got to the rapids. The boatman appeared to be enjoying the whole thing immensely, and was poling the boat along vigorously, periodically uttering wild, gibbon-like cries, apparently indicative of a *joie de vivre* which neither Jacquie nor I shared. As he was poling the boat from the back and we were sitting up towards the bows, it meant that we got the full benefit of the water when we struck the rapids. Great, hissing waves hit the prow of the canoe and spread themselves lavishly all over us, and within thirty seconds we were both so wet that we might just as well have swum up the rapids. To my astonishment, we eventually passed through the jagged chain of rocks unscathed and got into calmer water.

'Marvellous,' bellowed Chris, leaping up and down on the bank, 'now just do it once more so that we can get the close-ups.'

So once again, muttering unprintable things about our producer, we re-shot the rapids.

'Well,' said Jacquie after we had successfully passed through them for the second time, 'that's my lot. You can now take me back to the rest house so that I can change.'

Chris, who knew mutiny when he saw it, agreed to this.

'We'll leave Jacquie at the rest house,' he said, 'and then we'll go upstream and get a few more shots.'

Jim gave me an eloquent look.

Having dumped my damp and irritable wife back at the rest house, we chugged off upstream. After we had been travelling for about half an hour, the outboard motor suddenly made a strange series of popping noises and then died on us. In the pregnant silence that ensued, Jim whistled a few bars of 'For Those in Peril on the Sea'.

'What's the matter with it?' said Chris, glaring at the engine in an affronted fashion.

'It's stopped,' I said.

'I know that,' he said irritably, 'but why?'

The boatman, meanwhile, with an air of puzzled pre-occupation, had attacked the engine with a spanner and appeared to be disemboweling it. Presently, with a wide smile of pleasure, he produced a section of its internal anatomy which even I could see was irrevocably broken. He informed us that he would have to go back to the rest house in order to replace this vital part.

'Well, there's no sense in going with him,' said Chris, 'let's wait here.'

'One of us is going with him,' I said firmly. 'I've been caught on this sort of lark before. He'll get talking to his best friend's wife and that's the last we'll see of him for the next three days. I suggest you and I stay here, with the equipment, and Jim can go back with him.'

So we unloaded the equipment on to a sandbank and watched Jim being paddled downstream.

Chris and I were squatting on our haunches on the sand-bank, with our backs to the river, deeply immersed in discussing the film sequence we hoped to obtain if and when Jim returned with the canoe. We were taking absolutely no notice of our surroundings, so in consequence what happened next came as a considerable shock to us both. I half turned my head to flip my cigarette into the river and there, some fifteen feet away and swimming towards us at a rate of knots, was an exceptionally large and lethal looking King Cobra. He must have been about eight feet long, and his head and neck protruded a good six inches above the water; he had large, glittering eyes and from their expression I judged him to be of an irascible nature. If he kept on his present course, he would land on the sandbank exactly between Chris and myself. Ardent naturalist though I am, I felt that to have a King Cobra on such intimate terms was an experience I could well do without.

'Look out!' I shouted, and leapt to my feet. Chris, after darting one horrified glance over his shoulder, did likewise and we both retreated hurriedly up the sandbank.

Now this is where, according to all the best jungle literature, the King Cobra, hissing malevolently, should have hurled

himself at us and flung several coils round Chris's body and then, just as he was about to sink his fangs into Chris's throbbing jugular vein, I should have shot its head off with my revolver. I am sure this is what *would* have happened if it had not been for three things: firstly I had no revolver, secondly the cobra had obviously not read the right sort of jungle literature, and thirdly he seemed as horrified by our presence as we were by his. He had been swimming along quietly, minding his own business, towards a nice, friendly sandbank on which appeared to be a couple of decaying tree trunks. Then suddenly, to his horror, the tree trunks had turned into a couple of human beings! If a snake can be said to have an expression, then that cobra looked exceedingly astonished. He clapped on all his brakes and came to a standstill, reared himself a foot or so out of the water and stared at us for a brief second. I took comfort from the fact that all the herpetological literature I had read had informed me that death by cobra bite is comparatively painless, but the cobra had not the slightest intention of wasting good venom on us. He turned tail and shot off upstream as fast as he could swim, and about thirty yards away he made landfall on the bank and rushed into the forest as though hotly pursued.

'There you are,' I said to Chris, 'that just shows you how deadly these King Cobras are. An absolutely unprovoked attack!'

'What do you mean?' said Chris. 'He was as scared of us as we were of him.'

'Precisely,' I said, 'but the reputation for unprovoked attack is the thing that the King Cobra enjoys.'

'What a pity Jim was not here,' said Chris musingly, 'it would have given him something to moan about for the rest of the day.'

When Jim eventually returned with the canoe, we made our way two or three miles upstream and then landed to reconnoitre the forest to see if it would be suitable for the shots we had in mind. We had hardly gone more than a couple of hundred yards through the trees when to our right, on the crest of a hill, there broke out a cacophony of wild cries. Although basically similar to the gibbon's call, they were much louder and deeper and each cry ended in an odd, reverberating sound like somebody tapping on a drum with their fingertips.

'Siamang!' said the boatman, and Chris's eyes gleamed fanatically.

'Let's see if we can get close enough to try and get some shots of them,' he whispered.

We made our way cautiously up the little hill, trying to make as little noise as possible, but when carrying cumbersome equipment and surrounded by plants very heavily endowed with spikes and hooks, our progress was anything but silent. However, it seemed that the Siamangs were far too concerned with their choral practice to worry about us, for they sang continuously as we approached the trees in which we judged them to be. Just as we thought that we should be getting within sight of them, the singing stopped abruptly and the forest, by comparison, became so silent that our progress through the undergrowth sounded like the approach of a couple of madcap tanks. Suddenly the boatman halted and pointed up into the trees with his machete.

'Siamang!' he said again, with an air of great satisfaction.

Some seventy feet above us, in the crown of a rather elegant tree, sat a group of five Siamangs. There was an adult male and female, two half grown ones and one baby. Their coal black fur gleamed in the sun and they were sitting nonchalantly on the branches with their long arms and slender hands droop-

ing languidly. It was the arrangement of the group that interested me: the male was sitting on a large branch facing the other four animals, who sat in a row on a branch a little below him and some twelve feet away. It looked exactly as though he was about to give a short and erudite lecture on early Siamang music. In case we should flatter ourselves that we had crept up on him unobserved, he periodically glanced down at us and raised his eyebrows as though he found our sweaty and dishevelled appearance somewhat distasteful. Eventually he seemed to get used to the idea that we had come to join his audience, so he turned his attention back to his family. Watching him through field-glasses, I saw him shuffle his bottom on the branch to get more comfortable, and then he opened his mouth and started to sing.

The first three or four cries were short and staccato, and the effect upon his throat was fascinating. With each cry his throat inflated more and more as he pumped air into his extraordinary gular sac which, as it inflated, gleamed fiery pink beneath his fur. When it was large enough to please him, he launched into the song proper and it was interesting to note that at the end of each verse, as it were, his sac would start deflating until the next verse pumped air into it again. It was obviously this strange vocal sac that produced the odd, drum-like tapping at the end of each verse, and I could only presume it was made by the sound of air being expelled from this soundbox. As soon as he had finished his song there was a short pause, while his family, who had been listening with rapt attention, gazed at him fixedly. Then the big female, one of the smaller ones, or occasionally even the baby, would utter a series of high-pitched staccato cries that sounded rather like applause and were presumably accepted as such by the male, for he would react to it by launching himself into yet another verse of his song. This went on for about a quarter of an hour, the family group inciting him to sing more every time he stopped, and each time he sang he displayed more and more symptoms of excitement; it was rather like watching a pop singer working himself up to a final burst of song for his fans. First he started reaching out with his long arms and snapping off leaves from the surrounding branches; then he bounded up and down on his bottom and the family's applause became even more vociferous. Carried away by this, his next action was to run up and down the branch, his arms crooked and his hands dangling in that lovely pansy way that gibbons have; the family group grew positively ecstatic over this. Now he came to his finale and launched himself in a flying leap from the branch, dropped about thirty feet like a stone, his arms and legs completely relaxed and then, as you were almost sure he was hurtling to his doom, with a casual air he reached out a long arm, grabbed a passing branch, and swung there like a black, furry pendulum, singing his heart out.

Watching this grave but obviously happy choir of Siamangs gave me immense pleasure. They clearly took their music very seriously and enjoyed every minute of it. It was nice to feel that in that enormous section of protected forest, there would always be groups of Siamangs singing happily to each other in the bowers of green leaves.

CHAPTER 8

The Giants' Nursery

He skipped and he hopped, and he floundered and flopped,
Till fainting he fell to the ground.

Hunting of the Snark

MAKING FILMS is a weird business, and so I was not at all surprised to find myself, three days after we had left the National Park, standing on top of a step-ladder while Chris and Jim lay in the grass below me and Jacquie and various other individuals were spread around in a circle like fielders on a cricket pitch. The reason for this rather peculiar activity was one of the most curious animals that I have met.

We had set off across Malaya towards a place called Dungun on the east coast, in order to try to see one of the largest reptiles in the world, and en route we had got involved with a smaller, but equally interesting reptile. We had been travelling for some time over a series of hills, and the road consisted of the longest series of hair-pin bends through the forest that I can ever remember having travelled on. So numerous were they, and so close together, that Jim, who was lying in the back of the Land-Rover, presently asked whether we could stop. He lay there among the equipment looking like a Roman emperor, the effect being heightened by the fact that he was clasping to his bosom the largest pineapple that I have ever seen in my life, which we had purchased at a village a few miles back. His face was a startling shade of pea green.

'What on earth's the matter with you?' said Chris.

'I'm feeling sick,' said Jim sheepishly.

'Dear God!' said Chris. 'Is there nothing that doesn't make you feel sick?'

'Well, I can't help it,' said Jim aggrievedly, 'it's all these twists and turns. No sooner do I get my stomach in alignment than you go round another beastly bend.'

'Well, let's stop for a bit,' said Jacquie, 'and we can have lunch.'

Jim gave her an anguished look.

'Do you think I am in any condition for lunch?' he enquired.

'Well, I'm hungry,' said Jacquie callously.

So we unpacked the food and sat by the roadside, while Jim sat with averted eyes as we picnicked. Presently, stuffed with cold meat and pineapple, we lay back to relax and I noticed, in some trees a little way down the road, two birds which, from that distance, looked decidedly peculiar. Taking the field-glasses, I wandered down the road towards them and discovered that it was a pair of Racquet-Tailed Drongoes indulging in an abandoned bit of courtship in the tree tops. They are about the size of a blackbird, with curved crests and the two outer tail-feathers greatly elongated and ending in a round, racquet shaped piece of feathering; they are metallic blue-green below and glossy black above. They were not only dancing after each other through the branches, their tails streaming out behind them, but they were also flying up into the air and dive-bombing each other, and as they did so, the racquet shaped feathers on the end of their tails looked as though they were being pursued by two curious, round beetles. They would periodically utter a low, rather harsh chattering at each other.

While I was watching them, my attention was caught by a small, pale putty coloured lizard that was darting to and fro on the back of the trunk, lapping up the streams of tree ants that were ascending to their arboreal nest. He looked a dull and rather uninteresting little reptile and I was about to switch my field-glasses back to the Drongoes when he suddenly did something that made me, metaphorically speaking, jump about ten feet in the air: he protruded suddenly, from under his chin, a triangular white flap that looked rather like a sail. He kept flipping this in and out very rapidly for a few moments and then he hurled himself off the bark of the tree into the air. As he started falling towards the ground there suddenly blossomed, along each side of his body, a pair of butterfly-like wings, which he held out stiffly and, with their aid, glided nonchalantly to another tree some 150 feet away. I realised that the apparently uninteresting lizard that I had been just about to ignore was, in fact, one of the most exciting reptiles in the world, and one that I had always wanted to see. It rejoices in the name of *Draco volins*, the Flying Dragon, and I had been incessant in my enquiries about it ever since we had arrived in Malaya. Nobody had been able to tell me very much; you saw them, they said, in a vague sort of way that implied that you could spend fifty years in Malaya *without* seeing one, and then generally changed the subject. So there before me was a real, live Flying Dragon, a beast that I had given up all hopes of seeing. I uttered an anguished roar that brought the other three pelting down the road towards me, but as they reached me, *Draco volins* took off again and zoomed off into the forest.

'What's the matter?' enquired Jacquie, obviously under the impression that I had been bitten by something fatal.

'*Draco volins, Draco volins*,' I said incoherently.

They looked at me with a certain amount of curiosity.

'What,' enquired Jacquie, is a *Draco volins*?'

'That flying lizard job,' I said impatiently, 'there was one up here, zooming about from tree to tree.'

'Touch of the sun,' said Jim judiciously, 'had my suspicions when he first started talking about it.'

'I tell you it was here,' I said, 'it flew from *that* tree to *that* tree and then when you all came running up, it went zooming off into the forest.'

'A little lie down,' said Jim, 'that's what you need. I'll squeeze some pineapple juice on your brow.'

In spite of my protestations, they all seemed reluctant to believe my story, since they, too, had come to look upon the flying lizard as an almost mythical beast. So we continued on our journey and I made their lives a misery, talking about flying lizards all the way.

We eventually stopped at a small town for the night, where some charming people called the Allens had, to their credit, offered to put us up. After the preliminary politenesses had been exchanged, the conversation relapsed once again into talk of the flying lizard and Geoffrey Allen, a very competent animal photographer in his own right, listened to our acrimonious discussion with some puzzlement.

'Why,' he enquired at length, 'are you getting so fussed about the flying lizard?'

If he had not been my host, I would have felled him to the ground with a blow, but as he was my host and, moreover, was pouring me out an exceptionally large whisky, I resisted the impulse.

'I've always wanted to see a flying lizard,' I explained patiently. 'The moment I arrived here I questioned everybody very closely on the subject of flying lizards, with about as much result as asking questions in a Trappist Monastery. Then I saw one of the things on the road here and this set of morons that I'm forced to travel with refuse to believe me.'

'I don't see why,' said Geoffrey casually, 'the garden's full of them.'

'What!' I said incredulously. 'You mean *your* garden?'

'Yes,' said Geoffrey, 'dozens of them, flying about all day long.'

'It's the tropics,' said Jim earnestly to Chris, 'it gets them all in the end.'

'Do you think we would have a chance of filming them?' I asked Geoffrey.

'I should think so,' he said, 'although they are pretty agile. Anyway, you have a look at them tomorrow morning and see what you think.'

The following morning, at dawn, I dragged Jacquie, Jim and Chris into the garden, and there, to my delight, I found that Geoffrey had spoken nothing but the truth. There were flying lizards in every direction, gliding from tree to tree like paper darts. Jim, with the camera strapped round him, struggled to get some shots of them flying, while the rest of us beat the tree trunks with sticks to try to frighten the lizards in the direction of the camera. After a couple of hours of this, we were all sweaty and Jim had exposed about eighteen inches of film, which he assured us would be the finest shot of a completely blank sky that anybody had ever taken.

'It's no good,' he said, 'by the time I've found the damned thing in my viewfinder and focused, it's landed. I don't think we're ever going to be able to do it.'

'There's only one thing for it,' I said, 'and that is to catch one.'

'What do we do with it when we have caught it?' asked Chris.

'Well,' I said, 'then we can go upstairs in the house and

throw it out of the bedroom window when Jim says he is ready.'

'Um . . .' said Chris sceptically, 'well I suppose we can try.'

So, armed with bamboos with nooses of string on the end, we spent another couple of hours endeavouring to catch flying lizards. Eventually, having found some that were more imbecilic than others, we did succeed in catching two, then we repaired to the verandah for a well-earned drink before filming them. This gave me a chance to examine our captures closely.

The pouch under the throat was shaped rather like an elongated and slender strawberry; normally it lay folded back, so that it was invisible, but when the lizard wanted to display (and, as far as I could see, this white ornament was only used when guarding his territory), he apparently inflated it with air, so that it flashed up and down at about once a second. The wings were even more extraordinary: the rib bones of the reptile had become elongated and these supported the thin skin fabric of the wing, like the ribs of an umbrella. When not in use, the wings folded back along the sides of the body, again like a furled umbrella, and were so thin and fragile that they were not noticeable. The whole creature looked incredibly prehistoric and, watching it furl and unfurl its wings as you touched it, you could well understand how similar reptiles had gradually evolved into the birds that we know today.

When we had quenched our thirst and cooled off a bit, we set about organising the filming of our lizards. In order to get a really good shot of the flight and the wings, we needed the lizard silhouetted against the sky. This meant that Chris and Jim had to lie on the lawn with the cameras at the ready, while Jacquie, Geoffrey and his wife Betty stood well back in order to re-capture the lizard before it escaped. Having

got everybody in position, I then went up into the bedroom, extracted one of the lizards from the jam jar in which it was incarcerated and, on being given the signal from the supine cameramen below, I hurled it out into the air. Immediately, it spread its wings and glided down to land on the lawn, where it was smartly fielded by Geoffrey. The cameramen, however, were not pleased with the result, so once more I had to toil up to the bedroom and throw the lizard out of the window. Altogether we did this some twenty-five times, and both I and the lizards were getting a little bit bored and fragile round the edges, so we called a halt and drank some iced beer while we discussed the problem.

The chief difficulty was that throwing the lizard from the bedroom window allowed only a small area of sky against which it was silhouetted, so obviously the bedroom window was not the answer.

'How about a step-ladder?' Geoffrey suggested. 'Because then you could move it about wherever you wanted it.'

Fired with this idea, we went into Geoffrey's storeroom

and dug out a pair of ten-foot steps, which were rickety in the extreme. If anyone was watching us without knowing what we were trying to do, they would have been pardoned for thinking that Geoffrey's large and spacious garden was the grounds of the local mental home. Chris and I staggered along carrying the ungainly, giraffe-like body of the steps, preceded by Jim, who would periodically lie down on his back, and followed by Geoffrey, Jacquie and Betty, carrying various vital items of equipment and the two lizards in their jam jar. Eventually, after we had gone round the garden about three times, Jim picked himself a site and we erected the ladder and got ready for action. By this time it was mid-day and the whole of Malaya had reached that temperature at which the human body attains melting point.

Stripped to the waist and wearing a large and extremely ancient straw hat borrowed from Geoffrey, I clasped a flying lizard firmly in one hand and proceeded to mount the step-ladder. This groaned and creaked and swayed so that I was full of all the fears for my safety that must have beset an apprentice going round the Horn for the first time in a Windjammer. Making sure that the fielders were in position and that Chris and Jim were lying on their backs beneath me, I launched the flying lizard into the air. I was not able to witness its flight, owing to the fact that the ladder took a very dim view of any untoward movement and my masterly over-arm casting of the lizard made the whole structure sway alarmingly. By the time I had it under control, Chris was standing there, beaming at me.

'Excellent,' he said, 'but I think we will have to do it a few more times in order to get it exactly.'

I began to regret ever having mentioned flying lizards, for we spent the entire afternoon under the blistering sun, with me on top of the ladder, swaying to and fro like an extremely inept circus performer, hurling lizards into the air at intervals. But eventually Jim declared himself satisfied and we could retreat into the coolness of the house and have a shower, first having released our two stars. They, by this time, were so bored with the whole procedure that they did not even bother to run away but just sat on the branch of a tree, glaring at us.

As a matter of interest, the resulting film—which was excellent—occupied some fifteen seconds of screen time and furthermore, nobody wrote to compliment us on this achievement. I hope that the many people who aspire to being animal photographers will bear this chastening example in mind before they embark on their careers.

The art of travelling in Malaya is not to get bored with ferries. In most tropical countries the rivers and streams spread out as complicated and as intricate as the veins in a human body. To get to your destination, you may have to cross half a hundred of these; the shallow ones you drive through with gay abandon, ploughing up a great, discoloured fan of water with the nose of your vehicle; the slightly deeper ones you may have to be pulled across, depending on whether the Rain Gods have been kind to you; but the really wide, ponderous rivers, that look as though they have the consistency of glutinous sherry, can only be crossed by a ferry. Ferries, like bus services, vary in different parts of the world, but the extraordinary thing about the Malayan ferries is that they are always at the opposite bank when you arrive, and this means that you are in for at least a half-hour, if not a three-quarter hour, wait. Sometimes the tedium of this would be alleviated by the fact that on either side of the road where we had to park there would be delightful mangrove swamps, each mangrove standing on what appeared to be a twisted, basket-like 'hand' of roots, buried in most gorgeously

glutinous and evil smelling mud. This was the home of a
variety of things. If you were near the sea, and the water was
brackish, you would get the Mudskippers, those extraordinary
fish whose heads look so like a hippopotamus—indeed, their
behaviour is very hippo-like, for with their protuberant eyes,
they can lie on the surface of the water and see what is going
on while revealing the minimum of their body. But the
Mudskippers have another ability which, when you see them
for the first time, is apt to cause alarm and despondency should
you be one of those people who imagine that the right place
for a fish is below water. The smooth, skating-rink-like
surface of the mud below the mangrove roots is, as far as
they are concerned, an ideal terrain, and they haul themselves out of the water and skitter about on the mud, occasionally even climbing up on to the basket-like roots of the
mangroves.

The other most obvious inhabitants of this odoriferous
terrain are the Calling Crabs, who dig their burrows in the
mud and are as multi-coloured as butterflies. In the tropics
you always get those damp sections of bank along rivers
where the butterflies like to congregate to sip up the moisture;
these vast congregations sit there, sipping quietly, and
occasionally opening and closing their wings so that what is
normally a rather drab area of earth suddenly turns, momentarily, into the most flamboyant firework display. Calling
Crabs also fulfil this aesthetic function in the mangrove
swamps. They come out of their burrows and edge forward,
glowing in the sunlight, their one gigantic claw forever
moving, beckoning the female and threatening the male in
one economical gesture, stopping periodically to stuff dainty
portions of mud into their mouths, which they mumble
around to extract the algae on which they live. They look
ludicrously like somebody eating very daintily with chop-

sticks in a sewer. The effect is quite extraordinary; you walk up to a great, glistening sheet of mud and you are briefly aware of what appears to be little flashes of multi-coloured light that disappear down holes in the smooth surface. Then you crouch on your haunches and wait patiently and presently, out of one hole, and then another, and another, you see the claws appearing; slowly and with infinite caution, the crabs edge their way out of the safety of their burrows and pause to make sure the danger is gone. They glow like miniature lights in an armour of scarlet, purple, green and yellow, and even when they are immobile, searching for danger, there is still the nervous tic in the large claws, which flick gently back and forth. If you keep still enough, they eventually gain courage and scuttle further out on to the mud; first the braver ones venture out and, when they are feeding and apparently coming to no harm, the more timid ones suddenly flood out of their burrows, and before your eyes the drab, grey, smelly section of mud that you have been looking at suddenly becomes transformed into a kaleidoscopic Persian carpet. Indeed, it has all the charm of a kaleidoscope, for no sooner are you tired of one pattern of crabs than you raise a hand and immediately, like a magician, you have a smooth surface of shining grey mud in front of you. Their movement of retreat into their burrows is so fast that you can hardly follow it—it is rather like having a child's magic slate on which grows the most complicated and beautiful pattern of colours which you can wipe away with a stroke of your hand.

After our sixth or seventh ferry, the others, to my astonishment, started to display a singular lack of interest in the Calling Crabs and/or Mudskippers. They paced up and down, muttering to themselves and complaining bitterly about the length of time it took to get the ferry from one bank to another. In an effort to placate them I explained that the ferrymen were excusably slow because they were taking extra care. They greeted this explanation with a certain suspicion until I elaborated by saying that not two weeks ago a large bus, crammed to the gills with gay abandoned Malayans, had driven on to one of these ferries, which had then suddenly turned turtle and drowned three-quarters of the contents of the bus. Jim immediately wanted to know why we could not get to our destination by land.

It was not until we got to our fifteenth ferry that we had any indication that the reptile we had travelled so far to see did, in fact, exist. The ferry took slightly longer than normal to reach us and we had exhausted the possibilities of the Calling Crabs in the surrounding mud. I noticed that at one side of the road there was a small hut, into which everyone was constantly diving and reappearing with refreshing looking bottles in their hands. I suggested to Jacquie that we investigate this phenomenon, as we were all, by that time, in urgent need of some liquid refreshment. It was too much to hope, I thought, that this palm-leaf hut would contain anything as exotic as beer, but, as it was now midday and we had been travelling for some hours, I was quite prepared to make do with a Coca-Cola. We entered the little hut and, to my astonishment, I found that inside was a well-laid-out shop, including a large deep freeze that was humming away to itself and keeping a large batch of beer beautifully cool. While we were waiting to be served, I noticed on the edge of the counter a large plate in which reposed what appeared to be gigantic ping-pong balls that seemed very much the worse for wear.

'Look at those!' I said to Jacquie excitedly.

She surveyed them suspiciously.

'What are they?' she asked.

'They,' I said, picking one up, 'are the eggs of *Dermochelys Coriacea.*'

'What's that?' she asked.

'That is the creature that we have taken so much time, trouble and expense to come and see,' I said. 'This is a Leathery Turtle's egg.'

The Leathery Turtle is not only one of the largest, but one of the most interesting reptiles in the world. It can grow to a length of nine feet and weigh nearly a ton. Unlike the other members of the turtle and tortoise tribe, who have a hard, horny carapace, the Leathery Turtle's back is covered with skin, with a few protruding knobs of bone down the middle to show that it is related to the tortoises. Nobody knows very much about this large and rather sad creature; it feeds on fish and other sea food and occasionally on seaweed, and presumably it must have been, at one time, much more widespread than it is today. At the time that we were in Malaya, there were only three known breeding grounds for the Leathery Turtle: one in Puerto Rico, one in Ceylon and the one we were heading for, in Malaya. But, unfortunately for the Leathery Turtle, the fact that its eggs are so palatable had led to a wholesale exploitation of its breeding grounds in Puerto Rico and Ceylon, and indiscriminate collecting of the eggs had eventually driven off the turtles. So the Malayan beach at Dungun was the last place in the world where the nurseries of the Leathery Turtle could be found. I was anxious to see them for two reasons: firstly, because unless you catch a Leathery Turtle coming out on to the beach to lay its eggs, you do not stand a very great chance of *ever* seeing one; secondly, because the Malayan Government had just instituted an extremely sensible method of conservation and I was anxious to see how this was working.

The beach is some five miles long and a certain local

villager has always held the concession for harvesting the turtle eggs which, as they are considered such a delicacy, is an extremely lucrative business. But, like most people, the concessionaire was only interested in immediate profit and so he gave no thought to the fact that slowly, year by year, he was killing the turtles that laid the golden eggs. This is where the Government, with the help of the Malayan Nature Society, stepped in. They offered to purchase, every year, a certain number of nests at the current market price; these they then took and hatched out and released. By this method, not only was the future of the turtles secured, but also the ultimate livelihood of the man and his sons. On paper it looked to be one of the most sensible and progressive pieces of conservation that I had come across, but I knew from bitter experience that a piece of conservation legislation might look beautiful on paper but generally failed to operate successfully in fact.

Spurred on by the sight of the eggs, we continued on the last leg of our journey and eventually arrived at the small, neat town of Dungun. We had known, from various reports, that in order to be able to film the turtles on the beach we would have to have lights, for they only come up at night. How to provide sufficient light for photography on a beach some thirty or forty miles from the nearest power supply was a problem which had been kindly solved for us by the Malayan Agricultural Department, who had sent up to Dungun a short, almost circular electrician and a portable generator. He greeted us, blandly beaming, and said that he had booked us into the best place in the town, which was a Chinese hotel. It turned out to be clean and neat, if somewhat spartan, and by a stroke of good luck, Jacquie and I chose the bedroom next door to the bathroom.

I say good luck advisedly, for the proximity of the bathroom enabled me to do some scientific investigation into the cleanliness of the Chinese. The wall separating our room from the bathroom ended some six inches from the ceiling, so that every movement, every drop of water expended by the occupant, could be heard and measured. The first couple of people who used it had a brisk, but satisfactory swish down and left, whistling cheerfully, but the third man who entered the bathroom was of a different species.

He entered the bathroom at a run, as though hotly pursued by some enemy, and slammed and locked the door with such vigour that I thought the bolt might come off in his hand. This was enough to rivet my attention and I sat spellbound on the bed, listening to his activities. Having locked the door, he then spent the next five minutes or so breathing deeply, as though expecting his enemy to start breaking down the door at any minute. Was he, I wondered, being pursued by some strange Malayan Tong? Would his bloodstained corpse be found hanging from the towel rail when I next entered the bathroom? However, apparently his fears died down after a time, for he stopped his deep breathing exercises and proceeded to do what—I can only conclude—was to pat the bath. Strange, sonorous, cathedral-like notes floated over the partition as he banged vigorously at the porcelain. This went on for some time and I was just about to beat on the wall and suggest that this was the wrong way to escape observation from a pursuing Tong, when he stopped. His next action, so far as I could judge, was to scrub the floor with a dry scrubbing brush; this went on for a long time too. Having banged the bath and scrubbed the floor into a suitable condition, he then at last turned on the water. Absolute silence reigned except for the sound of the taps and I visualised him standing there, mute and terrified, staring at the filling bath.

After a quarter of an hour had passed, I began to get a little restive. Surely, I thought, no bath could be so capacious that it could contain that volume of water without overflowing. I looked uneasily at the base of our bedroom wall, but there was no sign of any liquid seeping through. Had he perhaps drowned? Ought I to go and knock on the door? Perhaps, having turned on the taps, he had slipped and fallen and knocked himself out and was now lying face down in the bath. My anxiety for his welfare was alleviated when he suddenly turned off the taps and then (and again I cannot be sure, since I did not witness this with my own eyes) apparently leapt into the bath from a height of some twenty feet. The boom and swish of water had to be heard to be believed. Jacquie and I were now completely spellbound by our mental visions of what was going on through the wall next door and we sat nervously on the edge of the bed, sipping beer and waiting for the next revelation. It was not long in coming. He proceeded to utter a series of loud, strangled noises reminiscent of an extremely satisfied Water Buffalo in a particularly succulent wallow, and he accompanied this by hurling vast quantities of water up in the air so that they fell back into the bath with a resounding splash. I am convinced, to this day, that he must have used a saucepan or some similar piece of equipment, as I am quite sure that the human hands, even if exceptionally large, are not capable of picking up that volume of water and throwing it into the air. As a matter of casual interest I had glanced at my watch when he first made his entry into the bathroom and, on looking at it again, I saw that he had been incarcerated in there for half an hour. He continued to snort and gurgle and hurl water about for three-quarters of an hour more by my watch.

'What on earth's he *doing*?' said Jacquie.

'He's probably an exceptionally large Chinese,' I suggested.

'But he can't be washing. He's just throwing water about.'

The noise went on unabated for another half-hour.

'He can't be washing all this time,' said Jacquie.

'Well, he's doing something,' I said. 'If you help me, we can push that chest of drawers over to the wall and I can climb up and peep through the hole.'

'You can't do that!' said Jacquie.

'Why not?' I said. 'This is a scientific investigation. I shall be able to make my fame and fortune by writing an article for the *Lancet*.'

'You can't go peeping over walls at people having baths,' said Jacquie firmly.

'Do you think it would help if I sang him a few bars of "Stormy Weather"?' I enquired.

'No,' she said, 'but I do wish I knew what he was doing.'

Oblivious of our macabre interest in his activities, the Chinese continued to splash and gurgle with all the verve of a drunken mermaid, and then suddenly all noise ceased.

'Ah,' said Jacquie, 'he's finished.'

'Either that or he's thrown all the water out of the bath,' I suggested.

There was a long and ominous silence, broken only by deep breathing from the bathroom. Then, so suddenly that it made us jump, he turned on the shower at full pitch and proceeded once more to snort and gurgle under this.

'It's no good,' I said. 'I must push the chest of drawers up to the wall and have a look. God knows, I like to spend a lot of time in the bath, but do you realise that he has been in there for nearly two hours?'

In spite of Jacquie's protests, I had got the chest of drawers three-quarters of the way across the room when, to my intense chagrin, the Chinese turned off the shower and proceeded to open the door and vacate the bathroom with such rapidity that I could only conclude he had sensed my manœuvre. I rushed to our bedroom door and flung it open, determined to at least catch a glimpse of this Asiatic water-baby, but there was absolutely no one to be seen.

The whole experience quite unnerved me, and for the rest of our time in that hotel, in between filming, I haunted the upstairs landing in the hopes of seeing this elusive and hygienic oriental. I even got the chest of drawers in position, with a pile of books on top, in readiness for his next dip, but the only person I managed to see over the wall was Chris, having a shower—a sight so repulsive that I gave up the experiment altogether.

That afternoon we took our circular electrician and his generator out to the turtle beach. This lay several miles from Dungun and near it was a small fishing village in which lived the egg collectors. The beach was a long one with dazzling white sand, fringed with palm trees. The egg collectors informed us that the turtles would not put in an appearance before seven o'clock, but any time after that we could expect them. Once the turtle was laying her eggs, nothing at all seemed to disturb her concentration; you could even touch her without it having the slightest effect, but should she become alarmed on her way up the beach or when she was in the middle of digging her hole, she would rush back to the sea and not reappear. This meant that, having spotted our turtle, we would have to make our way across the sand to wherever she was digging her nest, fix up the generator and then, as soon as she started to lay, switch on the lights and start filming. As there was a very large expanse of beach and there could be no guarantee which section of it would be chosen by the reptile, it meant that we might have to hump the generator at a smart trot for half a mile or so. We did an experimental run to see how it would turn out, and it was at this point that I decided that the use of the word 'portable' in connection with this generator was the most gross euphemism I had ever come across. To begin with, the thing seemed to weigh about a ton and it was furnished with two minute handles on which it was almost impossible to maintain one's grip. Add to this the average daily temperature in Malaya and the fact that you were sinking up to your ankles in loose sand at every step, and you were very soon reduced to a state bordering on hysteria.

We left the electrician and his fiendish contraption in the village and drove back to Dungun for dinner, then, at half past six, we piled ourselves and our equipment into the Land-Rover and drove down to the turtle beach. It was a beautifully warm, moonless night, the ideal sort of night for the turtles to come ashore. When we arrived at the village, we found the Headman, several egg collectors and our circular electrician all jumping up and down excitedly at the edge of the road and waving their arms about. Apparently a large female turtle had just made her appearance and was even now hauling herself up the beach some three hundred yards away. This was an unprecedented stroke of luck and so, groaning under the weight of the portable generator and the cameras, we hurried after the egg collector who had spotted the female. Presently, panting and sweating and covered with sand (for we had all fallen down at least once before we reached the spot), we arrived at where the turtle lay.

I knew they were big, but I had not been prepared for anything quite so massive. She lay on the sand like the hull of an overturned dinghy; her head was the size of a large dog's, with enormous, heavy lidded, filmstar eyes that gazed mournfully into space. With her hind flippers, that were curiously mobile and hand-like, she had scooped out a crater in the sand some four feet across and two feet deep. Very carefully cupping her flippers, she was scooping out the damp sand to make a nice, cup-shaped hollow for the reception of her eggs. The exertion of having hauled herself up the beach and of digging this hole, caused her to pant and wheeze distressingly, and periodically she would stop digging and have a rest, uttering, at the same time, a prolonged, shuddering sigh that was quite heartrending. The mucus that normally lubricated her eyes and protected them against the sea water, now flowed copiously from them. It trickled down her cheeks and hung there in long, shining, glutinous strands and this, combined with her heartrending sighs, gave the impression that she was suffering from a melancholy so deep and so anguished that nothing could possibly alleviate it. Her shell was very curious, for it had the colouring and texture of a well-dubbined saddle with just the curious line of little pyramid shaped nodules of bone running down the middle.

She dug on solidly for about half an hour and then, apparently satisfied, she shifted her position slightly so that her tail and rear end were directly over the hole. Then, without any apparent effort, she started to lay. The first egg dropped into the nest, gleaming white and sticky in the lamplight like a huge pearl. There was a slight pause and then there was a positive fusillade of eggs, dropping as rapidly as gigantic hailstones into the nest. Most of the eggs were about the size of a billiard ball but here and there there were some which were only the size of a ping-pong ball and others the size of a large marble. Whether these stunted eggs would ever have hatched is, I think, a moot point, but of the ninety-odd eggs she laid, there were at least ten or fifteen of these deformities. When she had finished laying, she started to shovel the sand back into the hole, using principally her hind flippers, and stopping every now and then to pat the sand down tight. When the eggs were well covered, her front flippers came into

play, and she used these with a scything movement to scoop
up the sand on her broad-bladed paddles and throw it behind
her, so that her hind flippers could stamp it into position.
When the hole was completely filled in, she shuffled her great
body over it, allowing her weight to do the final pile-driving
of packing the sand into position; then she hauled herself
forward a few feet and started hurling sand backwards with
her front flippers with complete abandon. At first I could not
quite see the point of this manoeuvre, until I realised that what
she was doing was camouflaging the nest, for a smooth,
flattened area on the beach would have been instantly notice-

able, whereas now, under this hail of loose sand, it very soon
became indistinguishable from the surrounding terrain. When
she was satisfied that she had obliterated all traces of her
presence, she started to haul her great, nine foot bulk down the
beach, a slow and laborious process which took her about
half an hour, interrupted by long rests during which she sighed
and gasped and blew bubbles, and the long chains of mucus
hanging from her eyes became more and more encrusted with
sand. Then she reached the very edge of the sea and a wave
broke and washed her face clean. She lay for a few minutes,

luxuriating in the feel of the water, and then slid forward across the wet sand. The waves broke over her and then suddenly lifted her, and from being a gigantic, ungainly creature, she became swift and agile. She turned on her side, waved one flipper at us in a rather saucy gesture of farewell and, with speed and grace, shot out to sea.

Several more turtles came out that night and so by about midnight we had obtained all the shots we wanted and, tired but happy, made our way back to Dungun.

The following morning we returned to the beach to see and film the conservation measures that were being taken to preserve the turtle. This scheme was quite a recent innovation and had only been in operation for one season prior to our arrival. The man in charge of the operation, from the Fisheries Department, explained the system to me. The nests, as I said before, were purchased at the current market price from the concessionaire; these nests were then carefully dug up and the eggs transported to a special, fenced off area of the beach. Here a new nest hole was dug at just the right depth, the eggs placed in it and then the sand carefully packed down on top of them: it was very important to try to simulate exactly the conditions of the real nest. Then each nest was marked with a little wooden cross on which was written the date on which the eggs were laid, the number of eggs, and later, the number that hatched. The result of this was that the fenced off area of the beach looked rather like a Lilliputian war cemetery, with its rows and rows of little wooden crosses solemnly stuck in the sand. They had buried, the previous year, ninety-five nests, which amounted to some eight thousand eggs, out of which more than three thousand had hatched successfully. In the normal course of events, when the baby turtles hatch, they dig their way to the surface and then rush down the beach as fast as they can and into the sea. By some curious, telepathic means, most of the ocean's predators such as sharks and barracudas seem to know when the succulent babies are about to hatch, and so they line the shallow water in a hungry barrier and the babies have to run the gauntlet through this barrier to survive. What with the large proportion of babies lost in this way, plus the fact that the eggs were being harvested in such quantity, the outlook for the Leathery Turtles was pretty grim. In order to circumnavigate the line of hungry sharks and barracudas, each of the little war graves was surrounded, when it neared the time of hatching, with a circle of chicken wire so that when the babies hatched, they could not make their way down the beach. They were then collected in buckets and tubs and taken on the Fisheries launch some two or three miles out to sea, where they were scattered over a wide area. In this way they stood a much greater chance of survival.

When they first hatch, the babies bear very little resemblance to their ponderous parents—some four inches long, they wear gay, pinstriped suits of bright green and yellow and are rather enchanting-looking little creatures. Nobody knows how long it takes one of these little pinstriped babies to grow to maturity, but one imagines that it must be in the neighbourhood of twenty to thirty years before they are old enough to come back to the beach of their birth and dig their own nests.

So far, this scheme has been a great success and I hope that it will continue to be so. The great, white beach at Rantau should always be a safe nursery for these giants of the sea.

Summing Up

He had softly and suddenly vanished away—
For the Snark *was* a Boojum, you see.
Hunting of the Snark

SO WE CAME TO THE END OF OUR JOURNEY, which
had taken us some 45,000 miles through three countries, and
during which we had met dozens of fascinating animals. I
feel that—as I have rather tended to concentrate on these
animals to the exclusion of everything else—I may have given
a rather lopsided and too glowing a picture of conservation.
I would like to try to remedy that now.

Firstly, what does conservation mean? It is not merely
the saving from extinction of such species as the Notornis, the
Leadbeater's Possum or the Leathery Turtle; this is important
work but it is only part of the problem. You cannot begin to
preserve any species of animal unless you preserve the habitat
in which it dwells. Disturb or destroy that habitat and you
will exterminate the species as surely as if you had shot it. So
conservation means that you have to preserve forest and grassland, river and lake, even the sea itself. This is vital not only
for the preservation of animal life generally, but for the future
existence of man himself—a point that seems to escape many
people.

We have inherited an incredibly beautiful and complex
garden, but the trouble is that we have been appallingly bad

gardeners. We have not bothered to acquaint ourselves with the simplest principles of gardening. By neglecting our garden, we are storing up for ourselves, in the not very distant future, a world catastrophe as bad as any atomic war, and we are doing it with all the bland complacency of an idiot child chopping up a Rembrandt with a pair of scissors. We go on, year after year, all over the world, creating dust bowls and erosion but cutting down forests and overgrazing our grasslands, polluting one of our most vital commodities— water—with industrial filth, and all the time we are breeding with the ferocity of the Brown Rat, and wondering why there is not enough food to go round. We now stand so aloof from nature that we think we are God. This has always been a dangerous supposition.

The attitude of the average person to the world he lives in is completely selfish. When I take people round to see my animals, one of the first questions they ask (unless the animal is cuddly and appealing) is, 'What use is it?' by which they mean, what use is it to them? To this one can only reply, 'What use is the Acropolis?' Does a creature have to be of direct material use to mankind in order to exist? By and large, by asking the question 'What use is it?' you are asking the animal to justify its existence without having justified your own.

The picture of conservation that I found in New Zealand, Australia and Malaya was distressingly familiar. Small bands of dedicated, underpaid and overworked individuals are fighting a battle against public apathy and political and big business chicanery. By and large people are only apathetic because they do not realise what is going on, but the most dangerous part of the problem is political apathy because it is only at top level that you can get things done. Most politicians would not risk their careers for the sake of conservation, because firstly they do not think it is important, and secondly they treat all conservationists with the disregard that they would display to an elderly spinster's ravings over her pet peke. A Cabinet Minister, no less, in New Zealand said to me that it did not matter if some albatrosses which nested on an island in the south deserted their colony. The reason he gave for this was that the island was so far south that no one interested in albatrosses could get down there anyway, so why worry? My reply was that there were a number of paintings and sculptures in Europe which I should probably never see, but I would not suggest destroying them on that score. But if you get this sort of attitude at Government level, what chance does the conservationist stand? People very complacently say, 'Oh, there are large national parks and the wildlife will be quite safe in those.' What very few people realise is that the greater majority of these national parks are not inviolate. Should, for example, gold or tin or diamonds be found in them, the Government could immediately allow mining in the area, thus destroying the whole point of the park. This is not just an alarmist attitude, because it has been done in the past. In fact, while I am writing this, there is a suggestion in New Zealand that mining activities take place on an island which is supposed to be one of the major sanctuaries and which is the last outpost for several unique species of bird. Again, in many areas animals have full protection on paper: you are not allowed to hunt or capture them. But this is purely paper protection and does not apply in fact for the simple reason that no machinery has been set up, either through apathy or through lack of funds, to implement the law. It is rather like saying you must not kill your neighbour but if you do we cannot stop you because we have no police force.

During the last few years there has been a growing awareness among people of the importance of preserving wildlife and its habitat. For a lot of species—the number, in fact, fills two fat volumes—this concern has come too late. In a great number of other cases there are species whose population has been cut down to such an extent that only a herculean effort can possibly save them.

All my life I have been extremely concerned about this problem. It seems to me that in many cases one could, by taking appropriate action, safeguard the creature in its natural habitat, but in many other cases this is an impossibility—or at least an impossibility at this moment. A good example of what I mean is the case of the Flightless Rail, of Inaccessible Island, one of the Tristan da Cunha group. This tiny little bird exists only on this island, which is about four square miles in area. It is found nowhere else in the world. On paper it is strictly protected, which is fine, but a friend of mine, a keen ornithologist who is in the navy, called in at Tristan da Cunha on his destroyer, and among the many souvenirs that the local people brought on board to sell to the sailors were rather badly stuffed Flightless Rails. Now the total world population of this bird cannot be more than a few hundred, since the size of their habitat would not support more, so what sort of damage is this depredation doing? There is no game warden in Tristan da Cunha to watch over the Flightless Rail; it would be completely impractical to have one. Yet, on that minute speck of land, the accidental introduction of rats or pigs or cats or any one of the human beings' henchmen, could destroy the Flightless Rail as completely as the Dodo in a matter of weeks or months. So there is your problem. In a case like this, how does one go about saving the rail? You can designate the island a sanctuary, but rats, pigs and cats unfortunately would be the last to hear of it, and unless there was somebody on the spot (which would cost money) you could not be certain that the sanctuary would be anything other than another airy paper promise. If, therefore, the rail is to be saved, it must be taken into safe custody in a place where it can live and breed without fear of human or animal predators.

The case of the Flightless Rail is not an isolated one; there are dozens of *hundreds* of species all over the world which are in a similar predicament. Sometimes they are threatened by the fact that their habitat is being destroyed or they are being preyed upon by human beings to such an extent that they can no longer hold their own, or else they are threatened by the fact that in the country in which they live there is such a total ignorance of conservation that people just simply do not worry.

At one time, if you had suggested that these creatures should be rescued and kept and bred in captivity, you would have been shouted down by all the well-meaning but woolly-minded animal lovers who are fondly under the impression that an animal in the wild state leads an idyllic existence. But slowly even these people have come to realise that in certain cases this is the only way of saving a species. In the last hundred years there have been several spectacular examples of this. The Père David Deer, for instance, which was only known from the gardens of the Imperial Palace in Peking. After considerable difficulty (because the bamboo curtain in those days was even thicker than it is today) a few specimens of this remarkable deer were brought to Europe. It is just as well, because during the Boxer rebellion the herd in the Imperial Palace gardens was slaughtered and eaten. With much care and trouble, the late Duke of Bedford gathered together a few specimens dotted about in zoos in Europe and formed a small herd at Woburn Abbey. Over the years these have increased and now number some 400. Breeding pairs have been sent to most of the major zoos in the world and just recently a pair were actually sent back to China.

The same success story can be told of the European Bison, the Hawaiian Goose, the North American Bison and a great many others. The most recent and spectacular example was the case of the Arabian Oryx. Hunted and harried by Arabs in fast cars with machine-guns and even, very sportingly, hunted by 'plane, this beautiful creature was reduced in numbers to such an extent that it was quite obvious that it could not hold its own. There were no conservation laws to protect it and the Arabs were completely uninterested in the fact that it might become extinct. A few of the remnants of this species were caught and shipped to America, where they are successfully breeding. At some future date, should the attitude towards conservation in their native home change, breeding pairs can be sent back to re-populate the areas from which they have been exterminated.

When dealing with a species, people always delude themselves as to numbers. 'Oh, there are plenty of those,' is the usual phrase, simply because they happen to have seen 150 specimens at a given moment; it never seems to occur to them that those might be the only 150 specimens in existence. That you can eliminate even the most prolific species in a very short space of time, is exemplified by the Passenger Pigeon. This was found in North America in such numbers that it was probably the biggest concentration of birds known on earth. Some flocks were, at a conservative estimate, 2,230,272,000 birds strong. When they roosted, the weight of their numbers broke large branches off trees. There was some small justi-fication for saying that there were plenty of those! So they were shot unmercifully, because there were plenty of them, and their eggs and young were taken in vast quantities, because there were plenty of them. The last Passenger Pigeon died, celibate, in the Cincinnati Zoo in 1914. If somebody had

had the interest to take four or five specimens of this prolific species and breed them in captivity, the Passenger Pigeon would not be extinct. Then, as the attitude towards conservation changed in North America, it could have been re-introduced to its former range.

It is only quite recently that conservationists and zoological gardens have become aware of these facts of life, and the majority of zoos now realise that their function is no longer to exist as places of interest and amusement, but that their primary object must be to keep and breed these threatened species. They must, in fact, act as reservoirs to prevent hundreds of animals from becoming extinct.

In 1959 I started a zoo in Jersey, in the Channel Islands, with just such an objective in mind. Once the zoo was established, I turned it into the Jersey Wildlife Preservation Trust. The purposes of the Trust are quite straightforward: firstly, to try to build up breeding colonies of those species which, in their natural state, receive either no protection or merely token paper protection, thus ensuring that they do not vanish for ever. We live in hopes, at the same time, that eventually breeding pairs might be re-introduced to their country of origin. The second purpose is to try to explain the urgent need for conservation—but sensible conservation, based on what we know about the way the world functions and bearing in mind the needs of mankind. Although we are small, we are the very first zoo in the world to devote all our efforts to this sort of conservation and because we are small, we need your help.

If you enjoyed this book and have read and enjoyed some of my other books, then you will realise that it is the animals that have made it enjoyable. I am now asking *you* to help *me* to save some of these animals. You might never, in your lifetime, see the creatures that you are helping, but does this matter? Do you feel cheated on Poppy Day because you cannot actually see the maimed victim that your half-crown is helping?

Unlike us, animals have no control over their future. They cannot ask for home rule, they cannot worry their M.P.s with their grievances, they cannot even get their unions to agree to a strike for better conditions. Their future and their very existence depend on us. The Jersey Wildlife Preservation Trust has created a sanctuary for the innumerable threatened species, a place where they can live and breed without fear of enemies—human or animal. Eventually, we hope, when conditions in their native countries permit, they and their offspring can be re-introduced to their natural habitat. In effect, then, we have created a sort of stationary Noah's Ark. The need for such work is terribly urgent. In the case of many animals, help in five or ten years will be too late—they will have vanished. In order to survive they need your help, but they need it now. By becoming a member of the Trust you will be helping them immeasurably, so put this book down and write to me at the Jersey Wildlife Preservation Trust, Les Augrès Manor, Trinity, Jersey, Channel Islands, and say you will join, and then get all your relatives and friends (even your enemies) to join as well. With your help dozens of species may be saved.